Curriculum Related Assessment,
Cummins and Bilingual Children

BILINGUAL EDUCATION AND BILINGUALISM

Series Editor
Professor Colin Baker, *University of Wales, Bangor*

Other Books in the Series

Building Bridges: Multilingual Resources for Children
    MULTILINGUAL RESOURCES FOR CHILDREN PROJECT
Foundations of Bilingual Education and Bilingualism
    COLIN BAKER
Language Minority Students in the Mainstream Classroom
    ANGELA L. CARRASQUILLO and VIVIAN RODRIGUEZ
A Parents' and Teachers' Guide to Bilingualism
    COLIN BAKER
Policy and Practice in Bilingual Education
    O. GARCIA and C. BAKER (eds)
Multicultural Child Care
    P. VEDDER, E. BOUWER and T. PELS
Teaching Science to Language Minority Students
    JUDITH W. ROSENTHAL
Working with Bilingual Children
    M.K. VERMA, K.P. CORRIGAN and S. FIRTH (eds)

Other Books of Interest

The Age Factor in Second Language Acquistion
    D. SINGLETON and Z. LENGYEL (eds)
Equality Matters
    H. CLAIRE, J. MAYBIN and J. SWANN (eds)
Language, Minority Education and Gender
    DAVID CORSON
Making Multicultural Education Work
    STEPHEN MAY

Please contact us for the latest book information:
Multilingual Matters Ltd, Frankfurt Lodge, Clevedon Hall,
Victoria Road, Clevedon, Avon, England, BS21 7SJ.

BILINGUAL EDUCATION AND BILINGUALISM 8
Series Editor: Colin Baker

Curriculum Related Assessment, Cummins and Bilingual Children

Edited by
Tony Cline and Norah Frederickson

MULTILINGUAL MATTERS LTD
Clevedon • Philadelphia • Adelaide

Library of Congress Cataloging in Publication Data

Curriculum Related Assessment, Cummins and Bilingual Children
Edited by Tony Cline and Norah Frederickson.
Bilingual Education and Bilingualism: 8
1. Linguistic minorities–Education–England–Evaluation. 2. Cummins, Jim, 1949–
3. Education, Bilingual–England. 4. Curriculum planning–England.
5. Bilingualism. 6. Language and publication–England. I. Cline, Tony.
II. Frederickson, Norah. III. Series.
LC3736.G6C87   1996
371.97′0942–dc20   95-23850

British Library Cataloguing in Publication Data

A CIP catalogue record for this book is available from the British Library.

ISBN 1-85359-271-4 (hbk)
ISBN 1-85359-270-6 (pbk)

Multilingual Matters Ltd

UK: Frankfurt Lodge, Clevedon Hall, Victoria Road, Clevedon, Avon BS21 7SJ.
USA: 1900 Frost Road, Suite 101, Bristol, PA 19007, USA.
Australia: P.O. Box 6025, 83 Gilles Street, Adelaide, SA 5000, Australia.

Typeset by Bookcraft, Stroud.
Printed and bound in Great Britain by WBC Book Manufacturers Ltd.

Contents

The Contributors

Olga Barradas, University of London Institute of Education.

Tony Cline, Department of Psychology, University of Luton.

Liz Filer, Southampton Middle School.

Norah Frederickson, Department of Psychology, University College London & Buckinghamshire County Psychological Service.

Athene Grimble, Portsmouth Infants School.

Deryn Hall, Language Support Service, London Borough of Tower Hamlets.

Michael Haworth, Leeds Educational Psychology Service.

John Joyce, Leeds Educational Psychology Service.

Constant Leung, School of English Language Teaching, Thames Valley University.

Alan Pratten, Leicestershire Educational Psychology Service.

Usha Rogers, Leicestershire Educational Psychology Service.

Ann Robson, London Borough of Wandsworth Educational Psychology Service.

Section 1: Introduction to the Model of Curriculum Related Assessment

Introduction

The bilingual children of the title are those children whose circumstances mean that they have to alternate between the use of two or more languages in the course of their everyday lives. They may not have a mature level of competence in both languages but they are going to need it if they are to communicate effectively with all those who figure importantly in their lives. In an age of mass transportation and mass migration the education services of all countries with an advanced economy are working with many more such children than in the past.

Jim Cummins has been a constant source of ideas to those working in this field across the world. He was born in Ireland and some of his early studies examined the consequences of Irish-English bilingualism and bilingual education. Most of his career has been spent in Canada, first in Alberta and then in Toronto. His studies and his ideas have had a very extensive influence on language planning and public policy, on the development of research and, above all, on teaching practices with children across the world whose families speak a minority language in their society. This book examines how one of his seminal ideas has been developed to improve methods of assessing and teaching bilingual children in a number of centres in different areas of England.

The editors and authors wish to acknowledge the important part that has been played in the development of their thinking both by colleagues in their own departments, schools and authorities and by other contributors and participants in the courses and workshops at the Department of Psychology in University College London where the book originated.

1 The Development of a Model of Curriculum Related Assessment

NORAH FREDERICKSON AND TONY CLINE

Some fundamental challenges that face teachers of all bilingual pupils

This book focuses on methods of educational assessment. It is as well to recognise at the outset that improvements in the educational assessment of bilingual pupils will not be achieved through improving methods of assessment alone. Action is also required at a more fundamental and general level in schools. It has sometimes been assumed that all that is required is the translation of existing materials so that children may have the opportunity of working in whichever of their languages is strongest. Alternatively, attempts have been made to devise appropriate new tests especially for this group of pupils. One of us has argued elsewhere that such measures can only be a part of a response to the challenge. Effective communication and suitable test content may be necessary for successful assessment, but they are not sufficient. For bilingual pupils in particular it is also essential that the context empowers their achievement. Meticulous assessment under other conditions simply lends authority to a process in which problems or advantages of the setting are interpreted as attributes in the child (Cline, 1993).

The first of the fundamental challenges for those working in multicultural schools is to learn more about the cultural background and first languages of pupils from linguistic minority communities. Basic knowledge and understanding are required at a general level to facilitate communication with all pupils from the various minority communities represented in the school. In addition, in the case of those individual children who face particular difficulties, it may be important for the key staff working with them to be aware of relevant personal history and background (such as length of periods spent overseas). It may be impossible to understand the children's classroom difficulties without that knowledge, and an effective practical plan for teaching may go awry if it does not take such factors into account.

The second fundamental challenge lies strictly outside the scope of this book but cannot be ignored altogether. This is the extent to which the school curriculum is ethnocentric in character. For example, in Britain it is a legal requirement that the curriculum in schools in the local authority and grant maintained sectors should encompass the National Curriculum as laid down in statutory orders. Yet there has been no commitment in recent Curriculum Orders to the ideal of education for cultural diversity. Prescriptions for the content of the Curriculum, subject by subject, ignore the particular needs of pupils from ethnic and linguistic minorities. However, the way in which the curriculum is delivered is wholly the responsibility of schools. Teachers of these groups of pupils may try to offset the narrow aims and content that have been imposed on them through the strategies used in their teaching (Verma and Pumfrey, 1994). For example, learning experiences may be selected to reflect the diversity of British society, to counter stereotypes of minority groups, and to enable pupils with a different cultural background to pursue interests relating to that culture in cross-curricular topic work (Cline and Frederickson, 1991, Unit 4). Some of the authors of chapters in this book illustrate how a simple model of curriculum related assessment may contribute to the process. No approach to curriculum related assessment can ignore this challenge in the case of bilingual pupils.

Identifying the educational needs of bilingual pupils who make limited progress in school

When pupils from different language backgrounds are seen to be struggling with aspects of the curriculum, the first working hypothesis for their teachers will normally be that there is simply a problem of communication. They *could* master the relevant material if they were taught in their first language or if they were helped to improve their grasp of the current language of instruction. The first measure, therefore, is to offer adult or peer tutoring or other tuition in a community language or to arrange additional language support in English. But some children continue to experience difficulties in spite of such measures. Then the question arises as to whether they may have 'genuine' learning difficulties rather than just a problem over language.

Often this question is conceived as a choice between two contrasting alternatives: *either* the pupil's difficulties arise simply from a lack of knowledge of or confidence in English, the main language of the classroom, *or* there are deep-seated and wide-ranging learning difficulties independent of the child's language background. It seems most unlikely that thinking in these stark either-or terms is a helpful way of approaching the issue. As noted by Wright (1991), there is a considerable range of possible factors that might be playing a part in creating the children's difficulties. For example, do they experience the ethos or curriculum of the school as challenging and alien rather than welcoming and accommodating? Do they have a good conversational level of English which has misled teachers into setting tasks too abstract for their current language level? Have they missed many experiences that others in the class have had? Are they learning now at an appropriate rate and slowly catching up? Perhaps all they need is a little more time? Are they subject to particular environmental stress, including experience of racism? And so on. It is likely, in fact, that in most cases the causes of the child's current learning problems will have developed from a complex interaction involving several minor sources of difficulty. Children from ethnic and linguistic minorities face a wider range of alternative possible sources of stress and difficulty than other children. Thinking solely in terms of a stark choice between 'language problem' and 'limited learning ability' is a gross oversimplification. It is dangerous because it may lead to a simplistic and misleading strategy of assessment. For example, there may be a focus on the testing of children's general intelligence as the central method of determining whether they have special educational needs. There are two very serious problems with such a strategy: firstly, it ignores the many other factors, besides limited ability, that might be affecting the children's progress in school; secondly, it relies on using tests that were devised for one type of population to work with another population where some of the assumptions inherent in the tests are violated. It was because this second set of problems became widely recognised that curriculum related assessment grew in popularity as an approach for use with bilingual pupils. So the problems of using normative tests of intelligence in this context will be discussed in more detail.

Problems in using norm-referenced assessment materials in work with bilingual children

Early research employing normative intelligence tests with children from linguistic minorities led to the conclusion that learning two languages must disadvantage cognitive development. It was found that the children's scores on intelligence tests were lower, on average, than those of monolingual children (e.g. Saer, 1923). In retrospect this does not seem at all surprising, since the bilingual children were disadvantaged in the testing process itself, as they were being tested in their second language (McLaughlin, 1985). More recent research has suggested that specific *advantages* may accrue from bilingualism in childhood, advantages that can only be identified if more sensitive measures are used (Cummins and Swain, 1986).

Other research in the 70s indicated that normative tests were not reliable as an indicator of a bilingual child's abilities, at least when the child was a new immigrant. When tests were repeated regularly over an extended period, the scores of that group of children improved over time very much more than those of control children who were monolingual (Sharma, 1971; Ashby *et al*, 1970). When training or coaching was given, this group of children again improved their scores by a higher margin (Kroeger, 1978; Haynes, 1971). It thus emerged that intelligence tests of the traditional type particularly penalise children who have had limited opportunities to learn whatever is being tested. So an assessment strategy based on such tests will show significant social and cultural bias (Feuerstein, 1979).

Some commentators had suggested that this would only be true for tests that rely on language. If a nonverbal test were used, the language barrier would be overcome. But many of the results quoted above were obtained using nonverbal test materials (e.g. Sharma, 1971; Haynes, 1971). In some studies in which both verbal and nonverbal tests were used the disadvantage to immigrant pupils was *greater* on the nonverbal tests (e.g. McFie and Thompson, 1970).

Some elaborate solutions were proposed. One was to employ a dynamic assessment strategy and observe children's response to structured coaching and teaching. This appears to have considerable potential for work with bilingual children, but many serious technical problems remain (Hamers *et al*, 1993). Another solution was to employ different norms for children from each ethnic and linguistic community (Mercer, 1979). There are many problems with this approach in the USA and in any case it is difficult to envisage how such an approach could be applied to the even more diverse linguistic and cultural communities of British cities. In general, the alternative strategy of assessment that was viewed in the most optimistic terms as a possible way forward for work with bilingual children was curriculum related assessment.

Curriculum related assessment and bilingual children

Over the course of the past ten years CRA has gained widespread, and largely uncritical, acceptance as 'the answer' to many of these challenges facing teachers of bilingual children. Shapiro and Eckert's (1993) survey of a sample of American school psychologists revealed that only 16% of respondents did not consider CRA less biased than published standardised tests for assessing children from culturally diverse backgrounds. However consider Tucker's (1985) assertion that CRA

> properly includes *any* procedure that directly assesses student performance within the course content for the purpose of determining that student's instructional needs.

Given the breadth of this definition is it really credible that all such procedures in relation to any course content are equally acceptable? On the issue of course content it is clear that CRA can only be a non-discriminatory approach if the curriculum on which the assessment is based is non-discriminatory. In many cases this needs to be evaluated rather than merely assumed. For example McLaughlin (1985) points out that the developmental model of language used by schools tends to be based on white middle-class children's socialisation experiences. The assumptions embodied, about previous experiences at home and in the community, are reflected in the standard monolingual curriculum as well as in tests.[1]

It is also important to examine carefully the variety of procedures which can be used to directly assess student performance within the course content. These may range from approaches based on informal observation within the classroom to those based on highly structured, individually administered tasks to probe acquisition of taught material. The appropriateness of approaches at both ends of this continuum have been subject to criticism in recent years. Concern about the validity of informal teacher observation has led in some school districts in the United States (Louisiana for example) to a requirement for more systematic and structured data in order to counter discriminatory practices in referral to special education services. The Attorney for the plaintiffs in an influential court case (Luke S V Nix) quoted research which showed teachers to be biased in their judgements about children's attainment of teaching objectives in a way which underestimated the achievements of children from black and minority ethnic communities Galigan (1985). In a scathing attack upon 'the subjective and chaotic referral methods of individual teachers' the attorney pointed out that 'evidence abounds that regular teachers initiate referrals without documenting that alternative instructional strategies have been attempted and evaluated,' and concluded 'teachers have manifested a pervasive propensity to refer students who "bother them". The result is a haphazard, idiosyncratic referral method whereby different teachers refer different types of students because different student traits bother them.'

It would seem therefore that teacher judgments of children's achievement of teaching objectives based on informal observation represents one CRA procedure which is not to be recommended with bilingual pupils. It also suggests that schools need to examine with care the evidential bases for their assessments of bilingual pupils' progress. Additional structure may need to be provided such as that offered by the Record Sheets suggested in the last section of the Frederickson and Cline (1990) publication to aid Teacher Assessment of bilingual pupils' progress within the British National Curriculum.

The CRA procedures most commonly used in Britain over the past 15 years are those based on approaches from behavioural psychology (Solity and Bull, 1987). These typically have incorporated the use of *behavioural objectives, task analysis, precision teaching* and *direct instruction*, as described in Frederickson and Cline (1990). The general limitations of these approaches have been highlighted by a number of authors and their applicability in assessment work with bilingual children has been strongly challenged by Cummins (1984). The concerns of particular relevance to work with bilingual children are summarised below and readers are referred to Frederickson (1992) for a detailed review of the issues also relevant to monolingual children.

Cummins' (1984) main concern about behavioural objectives is that their prescriptiveness may restrict the recognition of cultural diversity. Behavioural objectives attempt to spell out what is meant by terms such as 'understand' by giving an unambiguous description of the behaviour you can accept as evidence of a child's understanding. However, Cummins (1984) draws our attention to the disadvantage that if we focus in on one, possibly ethnocentric, way of demonstrating understanding we may disqualify (or at least lose sensitivity to) different ways in which understanding may be expressed by children from different cultural backgrounds. For example if a teacher was assessing children's performance on the National Curriculum Attainment Target:

Science Attainment Target 3, Level 1 – Name or label the external parts of the human body e.g. arm/leg.

a relevant behavioural objective might be:

Pupils should be able to: Name arm, leg, head, stomach, hands, feet when the teacher points to part on their body and says 'What is this part of our body called? (Criterion: 6/6 correct, 2 consecutive days)

But what then of the Urdu speaking child who is still learning that arm and hand are differentiated in English, but who can name 10 other body parts?

Cummins (1984) further argues that the use of scripted *direct instruction* programmes such as DISTAR with bilingual special needs pupils may lead to a number of undesirable outcomes:

- It may decrease intrinsic motivation by establishing the teacher as the initiator and controller of linguistic interaction.
- Direct instruction tends to focus on superficial, low level responses and skills which are easy to express as behavioural objectives. The approach is not well designed to address the more important higher order generalisable conceptual skills which Cummins has shown to be a necessary foundation for educational success.
- Indeed, Cummins argues that the direct instruction approach with its emphasis upon teacher initiation and control may actually inhibit the active involvement of the child, which is necessary for the development of higher order cognitive and academic skills.

Cummins (1984), writing about bilingual pupils with special educational needs, has also expressed concerns about

the pitfalls associated with task analysis, at least in the way the procedure is usually interpreted.

Task analysis involves the analysis of learning goals to produce a hierarchically ordered sequence of well defined, discrete learning steps. Cummins urges that analysis of academic skills content in curriculum planning should be complemented by analysis of pupil performance. Knowledge of the causes of students' academic difficulties is highly relevant to decisions about appropriate intervention. He cites the Hawaiian Kamehameha programme as demonstrating that direct instruction of academic skills without knowing the causes of pupils' poor performance may be much less successful than instruction that is sensitive to the source of pupils' academic difficulties. The reduction in meaningful context which often results from breaking down knowledge or skills into less complex components that are taught more or less in isolation, may well make learning *more* difficult.

On the contrary Cummins argues that one of the best ways of assisting children to learn is to embed the knowledge or skill to be acquired as comprehensively as possible within a context which is meaningful to the child. In behavioural task analysis all of the emphasis is placed on the *curriculum*. The only aspect of the child which receives any consideration is their entry skills. Many would argue that this is a grossly inadequate basis for understanding learning interactions and designing learning experiences for children. Swann (1988) offers an illustration of the importance of considering how pupils bring their everyday understanding to bear on the curriculum. He described an exchange with a 5-year-old-girl who he had observed in a classroom drawing round a square. When he asked her to show him a 'side' of the square she was drawing round, the girl first placed several squares in a line touching each other and then, upon being asked again, pointed to the centre of the top of one of them. Swann found these responses rather puzzling until he considered what his request might have meant to the girl.

Her first response was to put some squares 'side by side', her second response was consistent with interpreting a side as a plane surface of an object, as in 'the side of the cupboard'.

Here it is argued that attention to the task should be balanced by equivalent attention to the child and the nature of his/her interaction with the task.

Solity (1993) contends that these criticisms fail to acknowledge the way the principles of precision teaching or direct instruction can be adapted as appropriate, independent of their specific methodologies. However, even if it is true that the *principles* of traditional CRA allow for flexible and adaptive modes of operation, the *practice* that is described in many published reports does not reflect that potential. For this reason we are satisfied that the criticisms made of the application of traditional CRA with bilingual pupils are valid. Cummins' criticisms are particularly compelling because they are derived from a clear theoretical basis focused on bilingual children's development of language proficiency. It is this same theoretical basis to which British educational psychologists and specialist teachers turned to guide their development of a new approach to CRA which would overcome the limitations identified in this section and address the challenges facing teachers of bilingual pupils which were identified earlier in this chapter. The next section will outline Cummins' theoretical account of bilingual language development and describe the way in which it has influenced the evolution of CRA practice with bilingual children.

Theories of language development

Theoretical approaches to the development of language proficiency have traditionally been unidimensional, focussing on one level of linguisitic analysis. Syntactic theories focus on developments in the child's mastery of grammatical features, explaining for example why mastery of passives, questions and negatives develops after mastery of statements phrased in the active voice. Semantic theories focus on development in the kind of meanings the child can understand and express. This recognises that utterances of the same grammatical form can be used to express different meanings. For example the utterance, 'Have you finished with this?' may be used to express the meanings, 'Hurry up, I want to use it' or 'I hope that you are going to tidy it away' – among many others. Pragmatic theories focus on developments in the range of functions for which communication is being used. Early in development, functions may be served by signs and gestures; later on words and phrases may be used in addition. The work of Tough (1977), which has been quite influential in the education of young children, identifies four language functions which were observed in children between the ages of 3 and 7 years: a directive function, where language is used to issue directions either to others or to oneself; an interpretive function, where language is used to communicate the perceived meaning of events; a projective function, where language is not tied to immediate experience but is used for example in predicting and imagining; and a relational function, where language is used in establishing and maintaining relations with others. A number of more recent theories look beyond the level of the sentence or the single utterance. Conversational or communicative competence theories focus on conversational exchanges using techniques such as discourse analysis while socio-linguistic theories give attention to the way in which language and communication is shaped by the social and cultural contexts in which they are used. These theories can be seen to have particular relevance to understanding bilingual language development and will be discussed further with reference to the critiques offered of Cummins' work from these perspectives.

At a theoretical level it can be argued that, focusing as they do on different aspects of language development and use, these different theoretical approaches are to some extent complementary. At a practical level we are likely to be more concerned about which represents the most useful level of analysis for particular purposes. It is perhaps not surprising that the theoretical frameworks developed to consider the language development of bilingual children have tended to address a number of these levels as opposed to attempting to treat language competence as a unitary construct. This is certainly true of the model of bilingual language development best known in educational circles which was developed by Cummins.

Cummins' theoretical framework

Cummins argued that language proficiency cannot be regarded as a unitary construct. His identification of two aspects of language proficiency, differentiated in terms of their functional relevance to the performance of cognitive and academic tasks, reflects his interest in educational issues. The two facets of language development which Cummins identified were originally called:

BICS – Basic Interpersonal Communicative Skills.

CALP – Cognitive/Academic Language Proficiency.

Cummins used an iceberg metaphor to illustrate this distinction (See Figure 1.1). BICS is the visible, formal aspects of language such as pronunciation, basic vocabulary, grammar. Whereas CALP is the less visible semantic and functional (pragmatic) aspects. These latter aspects of language have previously been rather neglected by educators, yet were clearly more relevant for cognitive and academic progress than were surface features.

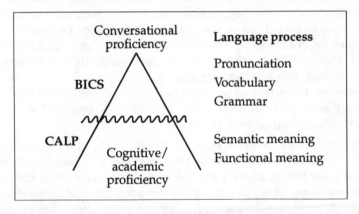

Figure 1.1 Surface and deeper levels of language proficiency

Cummins' basic hypothesis was that those aspects of language which make up CALP are of crucial significance to childrens' educational success, whereas those which comprise BICS are of relatively little importance. One finding of particular educational relevance is that relating to different rates of acquisition of BICS and CALP in the course of second language learning. Cummins (1984) reports that second language learners may acquire a good level of fluency in conversational English within two years of starting to learn the language, but that five to seven years' exposure is generally required in order to develop verbal cognitive skills to the same level as native speakers. Canadian and U.S. research indicates that second language learners are typically discharged from English as a Second Language programmes on 'surface' language criteria within a two-year period, yet it is only in the later school grades that they attain age norms in academic skills. There is still quite widespread ignorance about these differential rates of acquisition of different aspects of language. This can have considerable dangers in that if a child appears relatively fluent in English, poor academic performance may be attributed to learning difficulties rather than the lack of appropriate language skills. However, the more educationally relevant CALP skills may still be at quite an early stage in their development, even though the child has achieved a reasonable level of basic conversational fluency.

There is substantial evidence which supports the utility of distinguishing the two dimensions of language proficiency, as Cummins does. However, there has been considerable disagreement on the nature of these dimensions and how they should be conceptualised and described. Originally BICS was frequently illustrated by reference to face to face communication in everyday routine situations. It was, therefore, sometimes misinterpreted as communicative language proficiency and consequently criticised by communicative competence theorists who argued that anything other than the most superficial interpersonal communication involves considerable cognitive demands. For example, a discussion on the merits of proportional representation could hardly be described as 'superficial and lacking in cognitive content'. Canale and Swain (1980) put this point of view clearly:

> Communication is understood as the exchange and negotiation of information between at least two individuals. Communication is interaction based, involves unpredictability and creativity in both form and message, takes place in discourse in socio cultural contexts which provide constraints on appropriate language use, always has a purpose and is judged successful or not on the basis of actual outcomes.

The concept of CALP has also received criticism. It was originally illustrated by reference to formal academic situations and has consequently been misinterpreted in a narrow way as cognitive language proficiency. The criticism in this case has come mainly from socio-linguists. They argued that socio-linguistic factors may play a much more important role in influencing educational achievement than the 'tip of the iceberg' status accorded them by Cummins. The socio-linguists point for example to

Labov's (1969) findings on the distorting socio-linguistic effects of particular situations. Thus black American children demonstrated very impoverished language skills in a situation where they were formally interviewed by a white interviewer, whereas when two such children were left together in the room with a rabbit they demonstrated a rich and complex language usage. The socio-linguists' point of view is also supported by the observation that the match of language form and function in everyday situations to the system required in the classroom is very much involved in academic outcomes. Figure 1.2 is taken from Wong Fillmore's (1983) observational studies in classrooms where he identified a range of language functions which 8- to 10-year-old children should be able to deal with in order to succeed educationally. It illustrates that the language skills required in order to achieve educational success are by no means

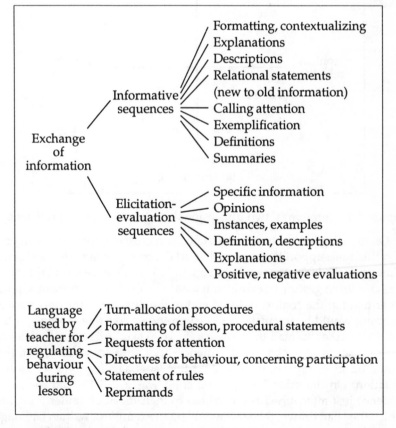

Figure 1.2 Language functions in comprehending classroom lessons (Wong Fillmore, 1983)

exclusively cognitive in nature.

Cummins responded to these criticisms, first of all by accepting that BICS includes only some salient, rapidly developed aspects of communicative competence such as pronunciation and fluency and does not include aspects such as social and pragmatic communication skills. Secondly, he acknowledged that CALP is also socially grounded and developed within a matrix of human interaction. He then went on to suggest that the distinction between BICS and CALP might more clearly and helpfully be conceptualised along the two dimensions illustrated in Figure 1.3.

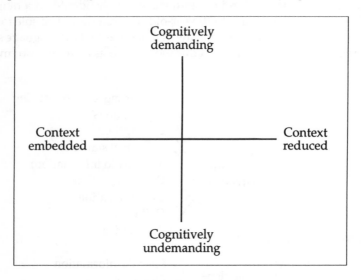

Figure 1.3 Cummings' two-dimensional model of language proficiency

On this diagram the horizontal dimension is used to indicate the degree of contextual support that is provided. At the context embedded end of the dimension the language would be embedded within a meaningful context and cues from gesture or expression would be likely to be present. On the other hand at the context reduced end of the dimension the only cues to meaning would be linguistic ones. To provide a concrete example; if the child was asked to read the sentence 'I like to skip' presented to them as one of a series of unconnected sentences in a sentence reading test, this would be an example of the use of written language in a context reduced situation. On the other hand, if the child was asked to read the same sentence just after it had been written to their dictation under a picture which they had drawn, then this would be an example of written language use embedded within a context that was meaningful to the child.

The vertical dimension indicates the level of cognitive demand placed upon the child by language used in any particular task or situation. Cummins regards cognitive demand as depending on both external factors and internal factors. External factors refer to those such as task complexity – where one could agree, for example, that addition is an easier and less complex mathematical operation than is multiplication. Internal factors refer to the familiarity and acceptability of the task to the child as well as the child's current proficiency. This highlights the point that tasks which are relatively cognitively undemanding for a native speaker may be highly cognitively demanding for a second language learner. This model therefore attempts to incorporate knowledge of what the child brings to the learning situation over and above their entry skills on the task in question.

Those aspects of language use which were formerly described as BICS, therefore, are located in this new model, within the bottom left hand quadrant, being involved in tasks which are cognitively undemanding and embedded in meaningful context. Those aspects of language use which were formerly described as CALP can be found in the top right hand quadrant where the child is engaged in cognitively demanding tasks where there is little supporting context.

Potential practical applications of Cummins' theoretical model were quickly identified by British educational psychologists. Desforges and Kerr (1984) visually located common everyday and classroom activities on the two dimensional framework, illustrating that the model could be used to identify tasks and situations in terms of the typical linguistic demands which they place upon the child. This graphical location of activities on the framework provided the stimulus for a working group of psychological service personnel meeting at University College London in 1989 to develop Deforges and Kerr's (1984) application in a dynamic way which could form the basis of a new approach to CRA. The outcome of this work was described in detail in Frederickson and Cline (1990). In summary it was suggested that in conducting a curriculum based assessment it could be helpful to locate on the matrix those tasks where the child was able to succeed and those tasks where success could not yet be achieved. It was then possible to build up a picture of the child's strengths and weaknesses, in terms of the level of cognitive demand with which they could cope in particular curriculum areas, and to establish the level of contextual and other support required for success in a range of different situations. Figure 1.4 indicates how the model was able to provide a starting point for conducting an assessment of individual children's progress in the curriculum within their specific classroom context. This illustration uses English Attainment Target 2 from the British National Curriculum.

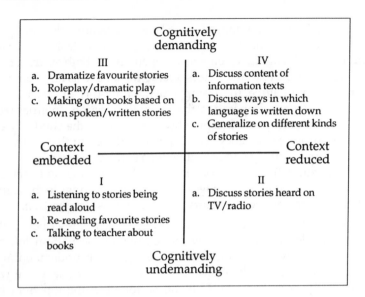

Figure 1.4 Primary English National Curriculum Attainment Target 2 (Reading), suggested programme of study, 5–7 year olds

This framework also appeared to offer a useful basis for differentiating classroom tasks and designing particular modifications by level (vertical axis) or method (horizontal axis) in promoting maximum access to the curriculum for bilingual pupils. Typically if a child is experiencing difficulty with a particular activity the teacher may respond by making that activity easier – i.e. by reducing the level of cognitive demand. However, second language learners may well be able to cope with the cognitive complexity of the task but simply not yet have developed the language skills necessary for access. To reduce the complexity of the tasks in this situation would result in the children being provided with inappropriately easy work which did not stretch them intellectually. The Cummins framework suggests that the teacher can instead facilitate the bilingual child's access to the curriculum by retaining the level of cognitive complexity involved in the task but embedding the task in a meaningful context so that the child is then able, despite their as yet rather limited linguistic skills, to understand the nature of the task and what is required from them.

The workshop members suggested a number of ways in which this application of the Cummins framework might help teachers:

- by providing a framework for topic planning which would allow for differentiating classroom tasks and help to demonstrate learning

achieved at a variety of levels;
- by providing a classroom observation tool which could be used to structure the collection of information about an individual pupil within the context of a working classroom;
- as a means of analyzing the content of the school curriculum;
- as a means of formative assessment which has direct implications for future teaching programmes and tasks;
- as a means of contributing to summative assessment, recording levels of achievement possible with different amounts of contextual support;
- through informing the debate over perceived learning difficulties, helping to distinguish difficulty in coping with an age appropriate level of cognitive demand (learning difficulties) from need for a higher level of contextual support (level of second language development).

A survey of educators' evaluations of these ideas

The strategy described in the previous section was outlined in a set of 'working papers' that was published by the Department of Psychology at University College London (Frederickson and Cline, 1990). This in-house publication has been reprinted in short print runs three times and remains unique in the United Kingdom as an account of attempts to develop a strategy for curriculum related assessment that is specifically suited to the needs of bilingual children. By 1992 the Department had details of a large proportion of the purchasers over a two-year period. We surveyed this group to try to learn whether they had found the ideas in the book illuminating, whether they thought that the methods of working that it suggested were useful, and whether there were any particular methods that seemed to them worth further development. We were interested to find out how people had used the suggestions and for what purposes. We also wished to learn whether a booklet of that kind was the most effective way of disseminating this kind of information and whether there were outstanding needs for training in this field. The summary report here will focus on issues relating to the model and the assessment strategy and will not cover issues of dissemination and training.

About one in six of those who were sent a questionnaire responded. It is unlikely that the sample of 57 people who replied is representative of all purchasers, but a representative sample was not necessary for the achievement of our purposes in conducting the survey. The 57 respondents comprised 23 teachers in language support services and teachers in similar posts, 26 educational psychologists, 6 teachers in primary and secondary schools and general advisers and inspectors, and 2 people in other kinds of post. Four replies from librarians were not analysed as they were not able to reply to the central sections of the questionnaire on behalf of their readers. Whilst an examination of readership patterns was not the main aim of the survey, we were interested to learn that 86% of respondents who had read the booklet themselves reported that they had then shared it with colleagues or others. 39% had trained others using the booklet. 90% had found the model as described in the booklet easy to understand.

A key question probed how often respondents thought that various ideas covered in the booklet had been used in their own practice. 66% had frequently or occasionally employed the framework for assessment based on Cummins' model. The purposes they had found it useful for were diverse :[2]

As a framework for topic planning	20%
As a classroom observation tool	36%
As a means of analyzing curriculum content	42%
As a means of formative assessment	37%
As a means of contributing to summative assessment	27%
To inform debate over bilingual children's perceived learning difficulties	70%

Many respondents added their own comments. Typically these high-lighted the perceived value of the model and the need for further work. For example, the leader of a language support service wrote: 'One of the few pieces of jargon I have incorporated for general use in visiting schools is the phrase *context-embedded*. It is amazingly succinct and useful.' Accounts were given of the model being used in LEA guidelines for secondary schools on the teaching of English as a Second Language and in checkpoints for teachers about the Standard Assessment Tasks and Teacher Assessment arrangements for National Curriculum testing. Another Service Leader described the model as 'like a seam of gold waiting to be mined more extensively. But its message permeates our service because the insights are helpful and illuminating.'

Thus the survey confirmed some of the hopes of the framework that had been expressed earlier. Why should that be? It is helpful that the approach focuses on generating improvements in a child's performance in the classroom here and now, not on speculative changes in future settings. It is also helpful that it is an approach or a model rather than an instrument. It does not fall into the trap of pretending to be the holy grail. Rather, it fosters a process of close observation and flexible response that is supportive of good teaching practice in the classroom and of maintaining high expectations of all pupils. It is valuable that the approach is simple to understand and readily accessible. Its core ideas are familiar to all educators (and part of well-established practice in many fields). So it could help to foster improved communication between those from different specialist groups.

It should be noted that the approach has attracted some criticism. Solity (1993) has argued that the form of assessment which is described would be unlikely in practice to enable children to generalise and apply their learning. We do not accept this and, in refuting it, would cite as an example of good practice Figure 1.5 below (reproduced from Frederickson and Cline, 1990: 44) which was generated by a reception class teacher and educational psychologist following a science activity on magnets. The learning hierarchy implied by this figure extends beyond a concern with skills learning to encompass concept acquisition, application and generalisation also; consistent with taking the traditional behavioural model of task analysis and regarding it with new eyes – from a cognitive perspective (Frederickson and Cline, 1990: 23).

Solity (1993) made the further criticism that the classifications offered for determining task difficulty, (cognitively demanding/undemanding and context embedded/reduced) and the way these are related to the cultural background of children, make assumptions and predictions about children's learning which may create differential expectations based on ethnicity. However the framework is essentially designed to make teachers aware that they should neither ignore children's language(s) and cultural experiences in planning for their learning, nor rely on simplistic stereotypical assumptions. Rather, teachers are encouraged to consider for each pupil how their proficiency in English and other languages which they may speak or how their familiarity with particular materials and tasks may interact with the planned curriculum activities to increase or decrease the level of difficulty of these activities. The ultimate effect, therefore, should not be to create differential group expectations based on ethnicity, but to encourage those working with children in a classroom to be sensitive to the *individual* differences that are associated with linguistic and cultural diversity.

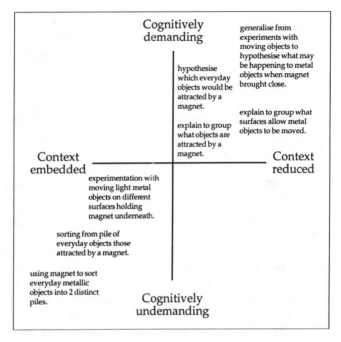

Figure 1.5

It is furthermore recognised that stereotypical under-expectation of children from minority linguistic and ethnic groups does occur, and accordingly teachers are urged not simply to substitute less cognitively demanding tasks (moving vertically in the framework) if difficulties are encountered, as would be suggested by a traditional approach to task analysis. Rather, teachers are encouraged first to move horizontally (left across the model) to ascertain whether the child is able to demonstrate success when given greater contextual support to their developing proficiency in English. In this way the Cummins framework offers an important new dimension to the curriculum related assessment of bilingual children.

At the same time there must be some caution. There may be problems about the model that limit the impact of the illumination it appears initially to offer – a flickering candle rather than a reliable searchlight? For example, there is some uncertainty about the degree to which the context-embedded/reduced dimension is independent of the cognitive complexity dimension. Also it is possible that the purposes for which the Cummins framework is useful may be fairly limited. At first sight the figures from the survey look impressive – a classroom observation tool for

36% of respondents, a means of analyzing curriculum content for 42%, a means of formative assessment for 37%. But the numbers were small, and the overwhelming majority of respondents (70%) found it useful to *inform debate* over bilingual children's perceived learning difficulties. Is it really more than a useful debating tool? We hope that reading Sections 2 and 3 of this book will enable the reader to give a positive answer to that question, aware of the limitations of the model but also aware of its potential for practical applications in schools.

Notes

1. The same issues arise with criterion-referenced assessment which is sometimes confused with curriculum-related assessment but involves a different approach to the task. In criterion-referenced assessment the pupil's performance is compared, in each area that is assessed, to a stated criterion or level of mastery (Frederickson, 1992).
2. Note that respondents could tick more than one purpose. Hence the percentages total more than 100.

References

Ashby, B., Morrison, A. and Butcher, H. J. (1970) The abilities and attainments of immigrant children. *Research in Education* 4, 73–80.

Canale, M. and Swain, M. (1980) Theoretical basis of communicative approaches to second language learning and testing. *Applied Linguistics* 1, 1–47.

Cline, T. (1993) Educational assessment of bilingual pupils: Getting the context right. *Educational and Child Psychology* 10 (4), 59–69.

Cline, T. and Frederickson, N. (1991) *Bilingual Pupils and the National Curriculum: Overcoming Difficulties in Teaching and Learning* (242pp.) London: University College London.

Cummins, J. (1984) *Bilingualism and Special Education: Issues in Assessment and Pedagogy*. Clevedon: Multilingual Matters.

Cummins, J. and Swain, M. (1986) *Bilingualism in Education: Aspects of Theory, Research and Practice*. London: Longman.

Desforges, M. and Kerr, T. (1984) Developing bilingual children's English in school. *Educational and Child Psychology* 1 (1), 68–80.

Feuerstein, R. (1979) *Instrumental Enrichment: An Intervention Program for Cognitive Modifiability*. Baltimore: University Park Press.

Frederickson, N. (1992) Curriculum-based assessment: Broadening the base. In T. Cline (ed.) *The Assessment of Special Educational Needs: International Perspectives* (pp.147–69). London: Routledge.

Frederickson, N. and Cline, T. (eds) (1990) *Curriculum-Related Assessment With Bilingual Children*. University College London.

Galigan, J.E. (1985) Psychoeducational testing: Turn out the lights, the party's over. *Exceptional Children* 52 (3), 288–99.

Hamers, J.H.M., Ruijssenaars, A.J.J.M. and Sijtsma, K. (1993) Learning potential assessment: Theoretical, methodological and practical issues. *Proceedings of European Conference on Learning Ability and Learning Potential Tests, Utrecht, 1991.*

Amsterdam: Swets and Zeitlinger.

Haynes, J.M. (1971) *Educational Assessment of Immigrant Pupils*. Windsor: NFER.

Kroeger, E. (1978) The role of training in the assessment of learning ability in migrant children: Overcoming lack in performance or competence? *British Journal of Educational Psychology* 48 (3), 361–2.

Labov, W. (1969) The logic of non-standard English. *Georgetown Monographs on Language and Linguistics* 22, 1–31.

McFie, J. and Thompson, J.A. (1970) Intellectual abilities of immigrant children. *British Journal of Educational Psychology*, 40 (3), 348–51.

McLaughlin, B. (1985) *Second Language Acquisition in Childhood. Second ed. Vol. 2.* New Jersey: Lawrence Erlbaum Associates.

Mercer, J.R. (1979) *'System of Multicultural Pluralistic Assessment'. (SOMPA) Technical Manual*. New York: Psychological Corporation.

Saer, D.J. (1923) The effect of bilingualism on intelligence. *British Journal of Psychology* 14, 25–38.

Shapiro, E.S. and Eckert, T.L. (1993) Curriculum-based assessment among school psychologists: Knowledge, use and attitudes. *Journal of School Psychology* 31, 375-83.

Sharma, R. (1971) The measured intelligence of immigrant children from the Indian subcontinent resident in Hertfordshire. PhD. thesis, University of London.

Solity, J. (1993) Assessment-through teaching: A case of mistaken identity. *Educational and Child Psychology* 10 (4), 27–47.

Solity, J. and Bull, S. (1987) *Special Needs: Bridging the Curriculum Gap*. Milton Keynes: Open University Press.

Swann, W. (1988) Integration or Differentiation? In G. Thomas and A. Feiler (eds) *Planning for Special Needs: A Whole School Approach*. Oxford: Blackwell.

Tough, J. (1977) *The Development of Meaning: A Study of Children's use of Language*. London: Allen Unwin.

Tucker, J. A. (1985) Curriculum-based assessment: An introduction. *Exceptional Children* 52 (3), 199–204.

Verma, G.K. and Pumfrey P.D. (ed.) (1994) *Cultural Diversity and the Curriculum*. Vol. 4. Falmer Press.

Wong Fillmore, L. (1983) Language minority students and school participation: What kind of English is needed? *Journal of Education* 164, 143–56.

Wright, A.K. (1991) The assessment of bilingual pupils with reported learning difficulties: A hypothesis-testing approach. In T. Cline and N. Frederickson (ed.) (1991) *Bilingual Pupils and The National Curriculum: Overcoming Difficulties in Teaching and Learning* (pp.185–92).

Section 2:
Applying the Cummins
Model in the Classroom

Introduction

The authors of chapters in this section of the book work in quite different settings in the ordinary school system with children and young people across a wide age range. They describe the distinctive ways in which they have found Cummins' framework useful in their particular contexts. The section opens with a challenging discussion by Constant Leung of processes of teaching and learning in the mainstream classroom. He takes the argument of the book forward with a more detailed analysis of the concepts of contextual support and cognitive demand that are central to Cummins' theoretical framework. He cautions against a naive reliance on context-embedding as the *exclusive* route to effective learning. His particular concern is to ensure that children who need to learn a second language are provided with classroom experiences that give them rich language learning opportunities whilst also making the curriculum content meaningful and accessible. In his analysis language is both 'context' and 'content' for the learner. Ultimately his account of the key components of contextual support in the classroom is intended to help teachers to match appropriate types of support to the needs of a particular student. Those needs will change over time as the student acquires new knowledge and new skills in both the language of the task and its content. It is emphasised that a strength of Cummins' framework is its dynamic character: as far as contextual support is concerned, the scaffolding that is essential for building work today may soon become redundant.

In Chapter 3 Athene Grimble and Liz Filer describe the use of the framework in the early years of the primary school with children aged 5–7. They show how the recording of classroom observations can be simplified to assist busy class teachers. For them the value of Cummins' model lies partly in the insights it offers about individual learners and partly in its adaptability for use by all those working with bilingual children. This may include, for example, a bilingual assistant who is not able to write in English. An important contribution that the framework can make in their eyes is to enable a class teacher to complement (and, if necessary, challenge) less satisfactory methods of assessment imposed by those outside the classroom – such as the use of formal tests that check word comprehension through context-reduced examples. Curriculum focused assessments such as those employed in the National Curriculum Standard Assessment Tasks may also be criticised – if, for example, in a subject such as Science they require a sophisticated knowledge of the language of the classroom rather than being designed to recognise understanding of key concepts in the curriculum communicated through nonverbal means.

Most illustrations of classroom work in this book concern children of primary school age. Some commentators have reported that teachers find the Cummins model difficult to put into practice with older secondary school students: at this level it is difficult to maintain the cognitive demands of a task while providing sufficient contextual support for, say, a recent refugee student (e.g. Jennings and Kerslake, 1994). Chapter 4 by Deryn Hall offers evidence that these problems may be overcome. This chapter, which concludes the second section of the book, is about the differentiation of the curriculum in secondary school classrooms. Hall summarises principles of good practice for teaching bilingual children on which there is a broad consensus not only in the U.K. but also in the U.S.A. (cf. McLeod, 1994). She then sets out to illustrate how the Cummins model has assisted in the implementation of these principles in a particular situation in East London. She sees the challenge facing teachers in this area as multi-faceted and holds out hopes for the Cummins model precisely because of its open, multi-dimensional character. Hall's examples are drawn from different subject fields in both the humanities and the sciences – 'more affective' and 'more conceptual' parts of the curriculum.

The appreciation of William Shakespeare's drama is a required component of the English curriculum in British secondary schools. Many of his story lines may have universal appeal, but the language of his dialogue is not easily accessible even to many young monolingual speakers of modern English, much less to those with a modest or recent command of the language. Materials originally developed by Claudine Field to facilitate access are described in detail in the text. Hall shows how Field's activities can be plotted onto Cummins' matrix in order to help teachers first to plan their use of the materials with particular groups of students and then to assess the students' levels of work on them. The simple, clear structure of the model is seen as an important attribute in its role as a shared tool for collaborative teamwork involving subject teaching specialists and language support specialists. At this level the complexity of subject knowledge can prove a barrier to effective teamwork with non-specialists unless a communication tool of this kind is available.

Further illustrations are offered from work in Science. Hall then takes forward the argument set in train by Leung on how some of the more common classroom cognitive processes may be mapped onto the Cummins framework. She concludes this section of the book by offering an evaluative overview of the practical utility of the model. There may be room for disagreement, she acknowledges, about the theoretical separation of the two major dimensions in the model, but, for her, its street credibility with hard-pressed teachers is an asset that has much greater importance than acknowledged 'academic' limitations.

References

Jennings, C. and Kerslake, H. (1994) Children in transition: work with bilingual learners. *Educational Psychology in Practice* 10 (3), 164–73.

McLeod, B. (ed.) (1994) *Language and Learning: Educating Linguistically Diverse Students*. New York: State University of New York Press.

2 Context, Content and Language

CONSTANT LEUNG

Introduction

The main purpose of this chapter is to interpret Cummins' theoretical framework from a mainstream classroom teaching and learning perspective. Contextual support has been hitherto considered separately from curriculum content in the professional literature. Here the concepts of context and cognitive demand (content) are developed as integrated components of a highly language-conscious pedagogy. Throughout the discussion it is assumed that second language learners are entitled to the same access to the mainstream curriculum as all other learners.

Conceptualising Language Use and Second Language Learning

Teachers have found Cummins' distinction between basic interpersonal communicative skills (BICS) and cognitive academic language proficiency (CALP) useful as a shorthand way of thinking about different types of language complexity and demand. In Cummins' theoretical framework of language proficiency, BICS and CALP can be seen in terms of context and cognitive demand or, more precisely, in terms of context and cognitive demand in various combinations. For example, indicating one's choice of food at the school canteen can be seen as an instance of BICS because there is immediate feedback (in terms of one's utterance/s being understood or not) and the language used is supported by a range of situational and contextual clues such as the food items on display. Furthermore the familiar and largely automatized utterances such as 'beans please' do not require a great deal of cognitive involvement. By contrast, working out the social class connections of different types of food consumption and meals in 19th century England from a set of written records in an individual (as opposed to pair or small group collaborative) writing assignment is an instance of CALP. In this task the language text involved is not supported by contextual clues; there is no immediate feedback on one's under-standing and the task itself is cognitively demanding in that it is not repetitively familiar and the writing activity is not automatized. Indeed both comprehension of the text and production of an essay depend, *inter alia*, heavily on knowledge of language itself. If the task is carried out in one's second language, the cognitive demand may be even greater.

It is generally understood that the BICS type of language use tends to occur in everyday communication and the CALP type of language use tends to occur in decontextualized formal academic learning activities. Cummins (1992:21) suggests that this approach to conceptualizing lan-guage proficiency has a pedagogical application:

> (An) ... application of the framework relates to language pedagogy. A major aim of schooling is to develop students' ability to manipulate and interpret cognitively demanding context-reduced text. The more initial reading and writing instruction can be embedded in a meaning-ful communicative context (i.e. related to the child's experience), the more successful it is likely to be. The same principle holds for L2 instruction. The more context-embedded the initial L2 input, the more comprehensible it is likely to be and, paradoxically, the more successful in ultimately developing L2 skills in context-reduced situations. A central reason why language minority students have often failed to develop high levels of L2 academic skills is because their initial instruction has emphasized context reduced communication insofar as instruction has been through English and unrelated to their prior out-of-school experience.

It is undoubtedly true that teaching and learning activities which are well supported by contextual cues such as pictures and realia and which are meaningful in terms of the learner's prior knowledge and experience are more comprehensible. There is, however, a need to recognise an important distinction. On the one hand, comprehension of meaning and purpose may be aided through increased contextual support. On the other hand, children need to learn to use a second language appropriately to carry out a learning task. Experience and research have shown that comprehension of meaning in context does not always automatically lead to language learning.[1] Understanding meaning in a contextually suppor-tive situation is not the starting point of some automatic transition to the development of an ability to process decontextualized language and meaning. Put differently, we cannot assume BICS will become CALP automatically in time. Teachers are familiar with the phenomenon of seemingly highly able and motivated second language learners finding it difficult to use English, their second language, appropriately and effectively to produce work when they have clearly understood the presentation of the task and the task itself.[2] It is also not unusual to find adult second language speakers who can understand task-related communication in English in a work context, say as a restaurant worker, but cannot cope with unexpected requests or an unfamiliar topic of conversation.

Perhaps it would be useful to see comprehension in context as a pre-requisite for learning in general, but by itself it is not synonymous with language learning. Comprehension in and through context is not sufficient for the learning of complex and decontextualized language use. The use of language in the teaching-learning process is an important part of any language teaching and learning agenda. In order to use Cummins' framework effectively in the classroom the concepts of context and cognitive demand have to be given greater elaboration.

Contextual Support

Teaching and learning activities can be seen as a meaning, sharing and making process jointly negotiated by the teacher and the learner. Learners have to be able to make sense of the teaching content for themselves. This process is more likely to produce a successful outcome if there is relevant and meaningful contextual support for the learner. Experience has shown that for contextual support to be effective, it has to be conceived, at least in part, from the point of view of the learner. This issue of perspective is important. What a teacher may consider to be helpful contextual support may turn out to be unnecessary, or worse, perplexing. For instance, the showing of pictures produced by the Third Reich authorities in Nazi Germany intended to portray certain physical characteristics of Jewish citizens in a derogatory manner as a way of illustrating racism (by the teacher) may not help the second language learner. The intended message may not be understood if s/he does not have any background knowledge of the significance of the supposedly undesirable characteristics. These characteristics may not even be noticed. This is not to suggest that such historical evidence should not be used. The point here is that the learner has to be able to make sense of the contextual support.

The concept of contextual support in the classroom is multifaceted. There are at least five aspects to be considered:

1. Learners' Background Knowledge about the Learning Tasks

A learner's initial perception and understanding of a learning situation and a learning task depend to a great extent on what relevant knowledge s/he already has. For instance, talking about and developing a story as part of a shared reading activity may not be a familiar idea to a five-year-old pupil at an early stage of learning English. S/he may not share this assumption about literacy practice with the teacher at this particular moment. It may well be that, for the time being, a teacher-led discussion based on or directly related to the pictures and text of the story may create the necessary contextual support for the learner to begin to engage with the task. Some or all of a second language learner's experience is encoded in her/his first language. The use of the learner's first language may also help to provide the necessary understanding because it may help to activate the learner's relevant background knowledge.[3] This aspect of contextual support is thus, in a sense, invisible. The support is embedded in the learning activity itself. The learning task itself can then be regarded as a part of the supportive context of learning.

2. Use of Drama, Visual/Audio Material and Realia

This is the aspect of contextual support which has been most widely understood and perhaps widely applied in the classroom. Learners' understanding of new information and skills can be enhanced by means of graphic and audio material of various kinds, e.g. pictures, charts, maps, drawings, tables, graphs, real objects and sound recordings. Emotional states, humour and attitudes (e.g. cynicism, disapproval and sarcasm) can be exemplified by drama activities. It is possible that some learners may find the support material difficult to understand, e.g. complex and unfamiliar graphics such as charts or speech recordings. Sometimes even seemingly simple support material assumes a degree of shared cultural or linguistic commonality which may or may not be there. It has been observed that, for instance, phonic worksheets showing letters of the alphabet may cause further puzzlement for some early stage second language learners. Similarly, pictures of objects such as an ink well may mean very little to some young beginner learners. In some cases they may not realise the value and usefulness of pictures and other visual images.[4] It is important that such contextual support does not become an additional obstacle.

3. Use of Language in the Classroom

Asking questions to check learner's comprehension of new information or a learning task and offering timely feedback on learner's responses can provide useful contextual support. These moments of teacher-pupil interaction also provide the opportunity for negotiated language use adjusted to the needs of the learner.[5] The use of the learner's first language may also be helpful. There is, however, a need to take into account the learner's perceptions and background assumptions. It is possible that the teacher's attention may cause unnecessary learner anxiety because this kind of teacher-learner interaction may be interpreted as a disguised form of 'testing' or the learner simply may not wish to be seen to need additional help in public. Sensitivity to the learner's perception is important.

4. Learning Styles and Personal Preferences

Learners have different views and preferences as to what constitutes a learning activity and how they would engage with it. Their views are influenced by previous learning experience, personality traits and current capacity to deal with learning tasks. Different tasks make different demands in terms of language and social skills. For instance, group discussion requires, among other things, turn taking skills which are socially and linguistically complex; it also requires the ability to handle unexpected, or even unfamiliar information, which may be linguistically beyond the learner's current repertoire. These may change over time. But at any one time a learner may display a preferred learning style; for instance some prefer to work collaboratively with peers and others choose to work on their own.[6] Task organisation is therefore part of the learning context which is open to conscious teacher manipulation.

5. Classroom Environment and School Culture

It is widely recognised that a learner's perception of how others in school regard them in terms of ability, achievement and personal worth is an important factor in determining the level of participation in learning and achievement. In general it has been observed that high expectation by others creates a conducive context for participation in learning. The corollary of this is in a situation of perceived low expectation and little peer support, the motivation to learn is likely to be low. Teachers are familiar with the scenario of seemingly able and motivated second language learners adopting the anti-learning and antagonistic behaviour and attitude of others when placed in a 'bottom' group, set or stream. This aspect of the learning context is, in one sense, invisible and yet all pervasive. It is not engendered by any one specific interaction between the learner and the teacher and other pupils or any particular learning activity; yet at any one moment it is part and parcel of the total learning context.[7]

It should be pointed out that these five aspects of context are distinct only in the analytical sense. In the classroom they are all part of the immediate reality. Teachers have to deal with them simultaneously. In terms of conscious teacher action the first four aspects – background knowledge, use of drama and visual/aural material, comprehension check and feedback and learning styles – are more open to immediate and direct intervention in the classroom. In a day to day sense teachers can take direct action to increase and enhance support in these aspects of their teaching. The aspect of context concerning classroom/school environment, teacher expectation and peer support requires collective and longer term school-wide development. It is, therefore, less open to and influenced by direct teacher intervention within the classroom teaching situation in the day to day sense.

Cognitive Demand and Content in Context

The concept of cognitive demand, just as in the case of context, has to embrace the learner's perspective. After all what is cognitively demanding for one learner may be totally undemanding for another who has already mastered the concepts involved. There is no question that teachers, using their knowledge and experience, can usually predict with a degree of accuracy whether a learning activity or task is cognitively demanding or not for a particular learner. The point here is that the concept of cognitive demand should not be solely defined by the teacher's judgement; it has to be learner-sensitive.

Cognitive demand is a conceptual abstraction. In the classroom situation cognitive demand is realized through learning tasks. Such tasks are normally derived from or generated by a syllabus or curriculum base. The National Curriculum Programmes of Study in the various subject areas are examples par excellence. Therefore cognitive demand has to be seen in terms of curriculum content. From the point of view of the second language learner in the mainstream classroom, the cognitive demand of any learning task is seen through the content knowledge and skills to be learned, e.g. the water cycle in geography, and through the English language used to express the content meaning, e.g. vocabulary items such as evaporation and grammar and discourse organisation expressing notions such as time and causal relationships. (In this sense language can be regarded both as a means of communication and as content.) The key question here is about what we can do to provide the requisite contextual support to render the content meaningful and accessible for the learner and at the same time provide language learning opportunities.

One of the major obstacles, from the point of view of the teacher trying to provide contextual support, is the range and the diversity of knowledge and skills in the different areas of the curriculum content. Science, for example, is generally held to embody a very different type of knowledge and skill than, say, literature or religious studies. At first sight it would seem that providing contextual support in the different areas of the curriculum requires a subject by subject and case by case approach. So, for instance, on the topic of the greenhouse effect in secondary science one may decide to provide an illustrated list for vocabulary items such as troposphere and to provide a series of drawings to show the formation of carbon dioxide, chlorofluorocarbons and other gases. And in a literature class one may choose to use action strips and a story map and so on. Over the years teachers have developed a great variety of effective classroom techniques to help their learners to understand and to do the learning tasks. It is, however, important to work out principled and practicable ways of providing contextual support which promote content and language learning across the different areas of the curriculum at the same time. This is an important point because neither the teacher nor the learner can afford to focus on just one aspect (i.e. either subject content or language) of the curriculum at a time.

One way of identifying similarities and establishing common themes in the different curriculum areas is to look at the thinking skills and semantic relationships which underpin the apparent surface differences in terms of factual information and skills. There is evidence to suggest that four common patterns of thinking pervade much of our everyday as well as academic experiences: comparison/contrast, problem/solution, cause/effect and description (listing). These patterns of thinking are referred to as top-level structures.[8] A moment's reflection will show that thinking about and working on comparison, for instance, occur in science as much as in social studies; indeed these are among the main activities in academic study in general. It is suggested that once the top-level structures (embodied in the curriculum content) have been identified, learning activities can be organised around tasks which help promote the appropriate thinking patterns. Teachers can also then make explicit how information and ideas are linked and expressed in spoken and written language and other forms of representation.

In a separate but complementary analysis Mohan (1986 and 1990) offers a theoretical framework which can be applied across the curriculum systematically. This framework consists of six types of knowledge or knowledge structures in three pairings:

Table 2.1 Knowledge structures

Background knowledge	Classification	Principles	Evaluation
Action situation	Description	Sequence	Choice

Each knowledge structure is associated with a particular thinking skill/s and is typically associated (in natural language) with identifiable linguistic expressions.[9] The following table shows some examples of the relationships between the knowledge structures and thinking skills:

Table 2.2 Relationships between knowledge structures and thinking skills

Knowledge structure	Thinking skill
Classification	Defining; understanding, applying and developing concepts and categories
Principles	Explaining and predicting; formulating and testing hypotheses; understanding and developing generalizations such as causes, effects, means, ends, rules
Evaluation	Judging; criticizing; forming and justifying preferences and opinions
Description	Observing; identifying; labelling; locating
Sequence	Ordering events; noting changes over time; planning action
Choice	Making decisions; selecting; identifying key issues

The first three of these knowledge structures, classification, principle and evaluation, are concerned with background or theoretical domains of knowledge. The second three of these knowledge structures, description, sequence and choice, can be mapped on to a great deal of the everyday classroom activities. For instance, a science activity involving testing, observing and noting the pH levels of different objects is a practical learning task; at the same time this learning task is related to the theoretical knowledge of acids and alkali. Knowledge of this kind is normally found in reference/text books or formal teaching or lectures. In this analysis, the practical activity can be seen as description and the theoretical knowledge can be seen as classification. The practical task of observing, measuring and charting the effects of exposure to varying amounts of air pollution over time on different building materials is related to the theoretical notion of explanation and prediction. The practical task concerns sequence and the theoretical knowledge concerns principle. The practical task of selecting one's favourite story as an entry for the best class story competition is related to the theoretical notion of making judgements and forming criticisms and preferences. The practical task is about choice and the theoretical knowledge is about evaluation.

From the point of view of working out a teaching agenda it is useful to note that these knowledge structures and thinking skills are typically encoded in and expressed through identifiable language forms, for instance:

Table 2.3 Language forms associated with thinking processes (adapted from Mohan, 1986:79[10])

Thinking process	Notional language
Observing/ Measuring/ Describing	Token examples: *This is an apple. Mary has three slices of bread. That apple is his. That is Mary's bread.* **Pointer words:** this/that **Verbs of class membership:** be **Verbs of possession:** have **Possessives:** his **Genitives:** Mary's **Referring to objects:** singular/plural nouns, count/mass nouns, part/whole, articles **Amount or quantity:** some/three **Unit nouns:** slice
Classification	Token example: *Apples are a kind of fruit.* **Generic forms:** apples/music **Species nouns:** kind/sort/class **Classification:** be/include/subsume

Teachers may not be interested in the formal analysis of language forms. The point here is that this kind of analysis shows that language use is related to the thinking process in a non-arbitrary way. In other words, the meanings embedded in the knowledge structures are expressed, to a great extent, through identifiable language forms. This is not to say that there is some mechanical one-to-one correspondence between a particular knowledge structure and a particular set of language forms. In the classroom situation, there is a need to differentiate between informal discussion and formal oral presentation, between making laboratory notes and writing a formal science report and so on. The context and the purpose of use will influence the selection of language forms. The crucial argument is that there is a principled way of looking at the content of a learning task and its attendant language use. After all teachers have an 'intuitive' knowledge of what is the 'right' language to use and make judgements about their learners' language use accordingly. The analysis suggested here will help the teacher to focus on the key language forms in a learning task with greater clarity; perhaps even more importantly this approach to content and language analysis is firmly grounded in the mainstream curriculum itself.

From the point of view of providing contextual support the most powerful aspect of Mohan's work is the argument that each of the knowledge structures can be represented graphically or visually. For instance, a text or a unit of information concerning different types of motor vehicles can be represented by a classification tree (see Figure 2.1).

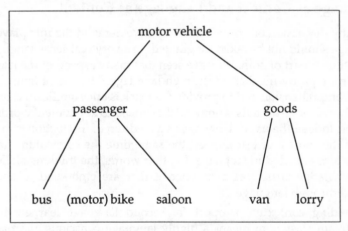

Figure 2.1 A classification tree for types of motor vehicle

Earlier we have already mentioned the use of visual representation as part of contextual support. Here the use of visual representation forms a clear and explicit link between the key concepts of context and cognitive demand. It has been found that this particular combination of analysis of content, knowledge and the use of visuals as contextual support in a principled way helps to lower the linguistic demand for the second language learners; it also allows them to understand and engage in cognitively demanding tasks which might otherwise be closed to them because of the linguistic complexities. Needless to say it is possible for a learning task to consist of more than one knowledge structure and thinking skill. The visuals can be used to form a key part of the classroom presentation of work and can be used as props or scaffolding devices for language learning. For instance, a classification tree such as the one above may be used as support for the forming of descriptive statements such as 'a van is a goods vehicle'; or it may be used as an information organiser for a piece of written discourse on types of motor vehicles. The actual focus and the level of the expected language outcome depend on the task and the learner's current knowledge. This is a matter for a teacher's professional judgement.

It is not being suggested that the only thinking patterns and skills worthy of attention are the ones mentioned here; nor is it being suggested that the context of the curriculum is entirely comprised of these patterns and skills. The point is that they occur frequently across all different areas of the curriculum. Indeed any examination of the National Curriculum content will show that they are central to most areas of study.

Language as Context and Language as Content

In any discussion on context and cognitive demand the role played by language should not be taken for granted. In a very real sense language is a constituent part of both. We have seen that many aspects of the learning context are partly manifested through language. The use of language to check comprehension and to provide feedback is one significant example. Even the use of visual aids is unavoidably linked to key content words and phrases. Indeed the use of language as a medium of instruction is in itself part of the context of learning. At the same time the curriculum content itself is also encoded in language. In other words, the thinking skills and the knowledge structures mentioned earlier are embodied in and expressed through language.

Providing contextual support for second language learners in the mainstream classroom means a highly language conscious approach to both the learning environment and the content to be learned. By insisting on the central role played by language in this way, the two analytical concepts of context and cognitive demand can be integrated practically in the classroom situation. Making the learning context more supportive and rendering the content cognitively meaningful and 'learnable' are no longer two separate issues. They are but two aspects of the same classroom interaction process of teaching and learning.

Content and Language Learning in Context

We have tried to elaborate on aspects of Cummins' theoretical framework with a view to applying it in the mainstream classroom. Perhaps it would be useful to summarize the key components of contextual support in the following form:

Table 2.4 A summary of the key components of contextual support

Aspect of context	Examples of classroom support
Learners' background knowledge	Using the learner's first language to activate relevant knowledge. Using supportive forms of teacher-pupil interaction such as text-based questions and answers to help learners begin to engage with a discussion task.
Use of drama and visuals	Using drama to show culturally-specific notions such as sorrow, humour and cynicism. Using graphics to show content meaning and to scaffold language use and practice.
Comprehension check and feedback	Asking questions to make sure that the learner has understood the teacher's meaning and to generate language use. Responding to the learner's apparent lack of understanding or knowledge by using alternative exposition to help engage with a task.
Learning styles and personal preferences	Giving the learner a specific role and language model in a collaborative/group work situation to reduce anxiety caused by lack of previous experience. Encouraging the use of first language to promote group discussion
Classroom environment and school culture	Publicly acknowledging a learner's progress in both content and language work to enhance a sense of achievement. Placing second language learners in a highly motivated group, set or stream to provide a hard working environment.

Throughout this discussion we have tried to emphasize the need to be learner sensitive and to look at the question of contextual support from the perspective of the learner's needs. The process of providing contextual support can be seen as an attempt to render cognitively demanding academic content and language more like everyday communication. The aim is, as Cummins argues, to enable learners to progress from only being able to use BICS to being able to function in a CALP type of communicative and learning situation. It is therefore necessarily the case that it is a dynamic and ever-changing process. What is appropriate contextual support and realistic expectation of learning outcome today may not be appropriate or sufficiently demanding tomorrow. As learners develop their knowledge and skills in both the content and language aspects, there is a need to constantly re-conceptualize contextual support.

Notes

1. Naturally-occurring use of language tends to be focused on meaning and not on form. Second language learners need to understand the meaning being communicated and to learn how to use the more formal aspects of language appropriately for different purposes. When the focus of the teacher and the learners is on the content meaning and on completing the task, they may not pay close attention to the form-function relationships in language. For instance, Swain (1991) cites classroom research evidence showing:
   a. in a history lesson a teacher using the future tense to talk about past events as a way of bringing history alive, and
   b. a student using the present tense in an answer concerning a past event without being remarked on or challenged by the teacher; the teacher was more concerned with the factual information.
   There is some evidence that comprehension does not require the same level of accurate grammatical knowledge as does production (speaking and writing). In any case, most second language learners, if they are to progress beyond the very basic communication type of language use, will require the opportunity to analyse and synthesize what they hear or read at some point and apply their knowledge and understanding in context. Spolsky (1989: Chap. 11) offers a discussion on this aspect of second language learning.
2. The term 'task' is used here in a non-technical way throughout this discussion. A task is generally realized at the same level as a unit or a topic within a programme of work, e.g. the devising of survey questionnaires in social studies. Under the National Curriculum most tasks can be derived from the specified subject content but the tasks themselves form the basis of much of what the teacher and the learners do together in the classroom. From our perspective, the task is the embodiment of the content knowledge and skill and the attendant language use; both are germane to this discussion. The concept of task has been the subject of a great deal of discussion in second language research and ESL/EFL teachers training literature. See Long and Crookes (1992) for a succinct account and Crookes and Gass (eds) (1993) for a more detailed discussion.

3. The idea of using current knowledge to facilitate new learning has been discussed extensively in the learning strategies literature. For a discussion see O'Malley and Chamot (1990: chap. 2). For a more second language specific discussion (working within the schema theory field) see Carrell and Eisterhold (1987).
4. The effective use by pupils of visual representation of information such as a graph or a table may not be taken for granted. For a discussion on the construction and use of visuals see Early and Tang (1991).
5. There is a substantial body of work which argues that language learning takes place when the learners are engaged in meaning negotiation. See Long (1983) and Allwright and Bailey (1991). There is some evidence that when learners are in a position to nominate the topic of conversation more new (for the learner) language forms are likely to emerge. See Ellis (1985) for a discussion. Pupil-pupil talk is an important aspect of classroom language use. For a brief discussion on types of pupil-pupil talk see Fisher (1993). It should be noted that this paper is not concerned with second language acquisition issues.
6. This is often the moment when the domain assumptions of the teacher and the learner about what constitutes a 'learning' task do not coincide. Under the National Curriculum the teacher is not entirely free to decide whether, for instance, taking an active part in a group discussion should be regarded as an appropriate task for a particular learner; many such tasks are prescribed. In the longer term the learner will have to make at least some attempt to satisfy the curriculum requirements if s/he is to succeed within the educational system. The point here is that the teacher has to be sensitively accommodating at any one time during the process of learning and adjustment. See Rees-Miller (1993) for a discussion. It should also be pointed out that co-operative or collaborative learning activities can be made to accommodate both individual and group work. For a discussion see Kessler (1992).
7. It is now widely accepted that school organisation and school ethos can and do have an impact on pupils' learning. For a discussion on ethnic minority pupils within the European Union context see Teunissen (1992).
8. For a discussion on the pedagogical application of top-level structures see Turner (1992). This account provides some classroom examples.
9. We follow the Hallidayan argument that language is used to convey meaning and that individual speakers make syntactic and vocabulary choices from their language according to the meaning being conveyed. In other words, the relationship between meaning and its manifestation in language, at the clause level and above, is not arbitrary. For an introduction to functional grammar see Halliday (1985).
10. For a full discussion on the knowledge framework see Mohan (1986, 1990). The presentation of the knowledge structures in three pairings is a slight departure from Mohan's exposition. The purpose is to make the meaning more immediately accessible and explicit in this discussion.

References

Allwright, R. and Bailey, K.M. (1991) *Focus on the Language Classroom*. Cambridge: Cambridge University Press.
Carrell, P.L. and Eisterhold, J.C. (1987) Schema theory and ESL reading pedagogy.

In M.H. Long and J.C. Richards (eds) *Methodology in TESOL*. Boston, MA: Heinle and Heinle Publishers.

Crookes, G. and Gass, S.M. (eds) (1993) *Tasks in a Pedagogic Context*. Clevedon, Multilingual Matters.

Cummins, J. (1992) Language proficiency, bilingualism and academic achievement. In P.A. Richard-Amato and M.A. Snow (eds) *The Multicultural Classroom*. New York: Longman.

Early, M. and Tang, G. (1991) Helping ESL students cope with content-based texts. *TESL Canada Journal* 8 (2), 34–43.

Ellis, R. (1985) Teacher-pupil interaction in second language development. In S.M. Gass and C.G. Madden (eds) *Input in Second Language Acquisition*. Rowley, MA: Newbury House.

Fisher, E. (1993) Distinctive features of pupil-pupil classroom talk and their relationship to learning. *Language and Education* 7 (4), 239–57.

Kessler, C. (ed.) (1992) *Cooperative Language Learning*. Englewood Cliffs, NJ: Prentice Hall Regents.

Long, M.H. (1983) Native speaker/non-native speaker conversation in the second language classroom. In M.A. Clarke and J. Handscombe (eds) *On TESOL '82: Pacific Perspectives on Language Learning and Teaching*. Washington, DC: TESOL.

Long, M.H. and Crookes, G. (1992) Three approaches to task-based syllabus design. *TESOL Quarterly* 26 (1), 27–56.

Mohan, B.A. (1986), *Language and Content*. Reading, MA: Addison-Wesley.

— (1990) LEP students and the integration of language and content: knowledge structures and tasks. Conference paper for the Office of Bilingual Education and Minority Affairs, U.S. Office of Education.

O'Malley, J.M. and Chamot, A.U. (1990) *Learning Strategies in Second Language Acquisition*. Cambridge: Cambridge University Press.

Rees-Miller, J. (1993) A critical appraisal of learner training: Theoretical bases and teaching implications. *TESOL Quarterly* 27 (4), 679–89.

Spolsky, B. (1989) *Conditions for Second Language Learning*. Oxford: Oxford University Press.

Swain, M. (1991) Manipulating and complementing content teaching to maximise second language learning. In R. Phillipson *et al.* (eds) *Foreign/Second Language Pedagogy Research*. Clevedon: Multilingual Matters.

Teunissen, F. (1992) Equality of educational opportunity for children from ethnic minority communities. In E. Reid and H. Reich (eds) *Breaking the Boundaries – Migrant Workers' Children in the EC*. Clevedon: Multilingual Matters.

Turner, A. (ed.) (1992) *Patterns of Thinking*. NSW, Australia: Primary English Teaching Association.

3 Using Curriculum Related Assessment Sheets in the Primary Classroom

ATHENE GRIMBLE AND LIZ FILER

Adapting the Published Assessment Sheets

When we first saw the original materials on curriculum related assessment for bilingual children from University College London, we thought that the Cummins framework might be of real practical value in the primary school classrooms where we worked. This chapter describes how we have used the assessment sheets over the years and how our views on them have changed.

The basic steps and questions in this approach are simple:

1. Look at the task and analyse the linguistic demands and cognitive demands.
2. Look at the linguistic demands in relation to the linguistic ability of the child.
3. Can the task be made more context embedded by making it more culturally relevant?
4. How else can the task be made more context embedded if this is necessary? e.g. by picture cues, demonstration, peer support.
5. Is the child grouped with supportive monolingual role models?
6. Has the child had experience of this type of task?

Here is an example from one of our classrooms which applies these steps to work in Science at Key Stage 1. We were focusing on Attainment Target 1, *Exploration of Science*, and the Statement of Attainment, *Describe and communicate their observations, ideally through talking in groups*. The child is a Year Two bilingual Punjabi/English girl who needs more experience of expressing her opinion in an English speaking group. The task was that the group was given six different balls and had to discover by experiment which ball bounced the most times in thirty seconds when dropped from a certain height. They had to consider if the number of bounces was affected by the material the ball was made of, its weight, size and texture, and they had to record their findings collaboratively. This sort of task was not new to the class. They were divided into four groups of six, and each group was given a different task.

The ball task

Look at the six balls. Try to decide what each one is made from. Is it hard or soft? Is it heavy or light? Write your answers here.

Ball number	Material	Hard or soft	Heavy or light
1			
2			
3			
4			
5			
6			

2) Put a marker on the wall at about the same height as you are. Drop each ball from the marker and count the number of bounces each one makes in 30 seconds.

3) Fill in the chart on the right for each ball by colouring one space for each bounce the ball made.

Figure 3.1 'Ball task' observation sheet, side one

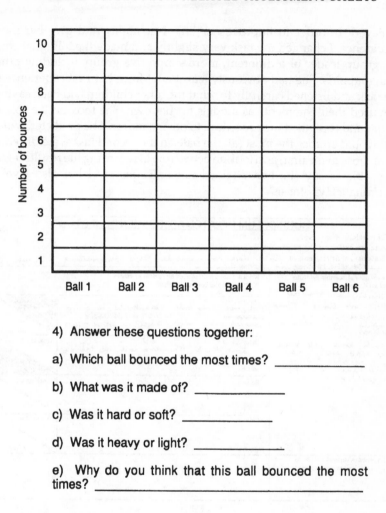

4) Answer these questions together:

a) Which ball bounced the most times? _____

b) What was it made of? _____

c) Was it hard or soft? _____

d) Was it heavy or light? _____

e) Why do you think that this ball bounced the most times? _____

Figure 3.2 'Ball task' observation sheet, side two

The outcome was that the bilingual child joined in but was reluctant to give her views or contribute in an active way. It was not that she did not understand the practical work, but she did not have the linguistic skills to join in with the confident monolingual children in the group. Also in her family it is normally men who make decisions and give instructions in practical areas outside the kitchen, so she was further disadvantaged by being grouped with more boys than girls. As the statement of attainment was 'communicate their observations', I could not say that it had been achieved. In order to improve her linguistic ability and give her more confidence, I changed the task very slightly and made the bilingual child the group leader of a different, more supportive group, including other bilingual girls. She had obviously learnt a lot from her first experience of the task and listened carefully to what the other children had been saying. She used their comments as models for her own. She took on the role of leader and explained the procedure to other children. She predicted which ball would bounce the most (all the balls in the second task were different from those in the first) and took an active role in recording the results. I was then able to say she had attained not only this level but also level 3 'Formulate Hypothesis'.

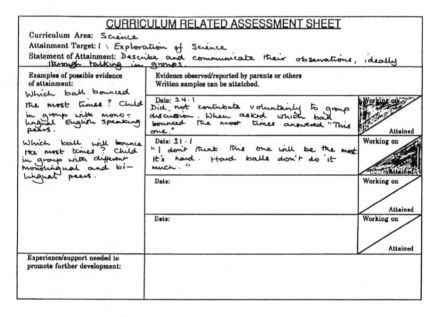

Figure 3.3 Assessment sheet for 'Ball task'

By using the curriculum related assessment sheet the first week I was able to understand the difficulty the child was having and design the task so that she was able to succeed.

This shows the usefulness of the curriculum related assessment sheets. However we do have criticisms of these sheets. They are very time consuming and detailed. For a class teacher, or even a class teacher working with an E2L teacher, these sheets would mean a lot of paper work at a time when teachers are feeling burdened and pressurised by paper work, assessment procedures and record keeping. We feel that the sheets as they stand at the moment may be useful only for children who are having difficulties. This type of detailed information would be useful in that situation. However, these sheets may not be so applicable for every child in the class. It is with this in mind that we have adapted the sheets to make them less time consuming and easier to use. The aim is to have one sheet for each level, not one sheet per statement of attainment as in the original form. As each statement of attainment is worked on and achieved, the teacher could fill in the form giving an example of how the statement of attainment was reached. This would show where the child was at and what he or she needed next. It could be used when reporting children's progress to their parents. Figure 3.4 shows the adapted sheet.

CURRICULUM RELATED ASSESSMENT SHEET		
Curriculum Area: English Attainment Target: ① Speaking and Listening. Level ③		
Examples of possible evidence of attainment:	Evidence observed/reported by parents or others Written samples can be attatched.	
Relate real or imaginary events in a connected narrative which conveys meaning to a group of pupils, the teacher, or a known adult.	Date:	Working on Attained
Convey accurately a simple message.	Date:	Working on Attained
Listen with an increased span of concentration to other children and adults, asking and responding to questions and commenting on what has been said.	Date:	Working on Attained
Give and receive and follow accurately precise instructions when pursuing a task individually or as a member of a group.	Date:	Working on Attained
Experience/support needed to promote further development:		

Figure 3.4 Adapted assessment sheet

This adapted sheet could be used very successfully with both bilingual and monolingual children and could be filled in by class teachers and ESL teachers working together. The six points above are still relevant to these adapted sheets. They would be filled in for Maths, Science and English initially. Now that the National Curriculum is being modified with fewer attainment targets, this type of fairly detailed record keeping and assessment procedure will become more viable. These sheets could be passed on from teacher to teacher. They would also be useful at the ages of transfer and could be passed on from school to school.

The Curriculum Related Assessment Sheets have also been used successfully in the context of a class teacher working alongside a bilingual assistant in the classroom. They provide a useful record of a child's achievements for both the class teacher and the bilingual assistant, and of strategies that may be used in order to promote learning. Their greatest advantage in these circumstances is that they can be completed in any language, enabling assessment to be made in the child's first language. These sheets provide a useful basis for discussion and collaborative work between the class teacher and bilingual assistants, and remove the necessity for the bilingual assistant to be able to write in English – a barrier that sometimes exists.

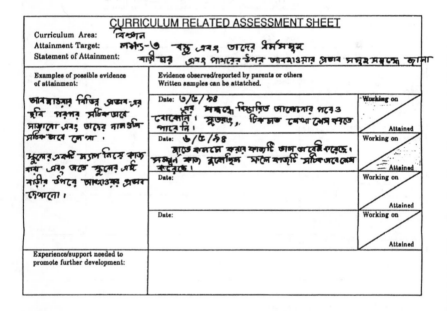

Figure 3.5 Assessment sheet completed in Bangla

The example shown above was completed by the bilingual assistant immediately after the tasks had been worked through by the child. She was happy to fill out this record sheet and found it easy to do so. The tasks were both discussed and explained to the pupil in Bangla by the bilingual assistant. The actual written work was carried out in English. After the first task was completed, the bilingual assistant and I discussed whether or not

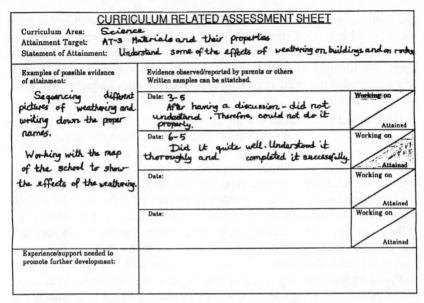

Figure 3.6 Assessment sheet on the weathering of rocks

the pupil had really achieved the statement of attainment, and decided he had not. We therefore planned a practical activity that the child could do with the bilingual assistant, and that would enable him to achieve that statement of attainment. The first activity involved the child in sequencing a series of pictures that showed the stages of weathering on rocks. He also needed to use words such as 'erosion', 'weathering', and 'cracks', to describe what was happening in each picture. The second activity involved the pupil and the bilingual assistant walking around the school buildings and grounds with a map, looking for evidence of weathering and recording it on the map. The child was able to complete this task successfully as the record sheet shows.

Other Methods Currently Used to Assess and Monitor the Progress of Bilingual Learners

Standardised Tests

The Cummins model shows the danger of using certain standardised tests with bilingual pupils. My school has been using the 'British Picture Vocabulary Test' with both bilingual and monolingual pupils. This test is designed to test the level of a child's vocabulary attainment and can, in theory, be used in any language. It involves the pupil being told a word and then choosing from a series of four pictures one that matches the given word. We have used this test across the ability range with a group of bilingual and monolingual learners. Without exception the bilingual learners achieved low results when using this test, even when the test was administered in the child's first language. No bilingual learner scored more than 50 per cent.

Undoubtedly vocabulary is an important factor in any child's educational achievement, and a bilingual child may not have the same range of English vocabulary as a monolingual English speaker, particularly if English is not spoken at home. Even so, we felt that this did not fully explain why even bilingual learners who are fluent English speakers should achieve poor results in this and other standardised tests. In order to fully understand these results we went back to the Cummins model. We looked at the possible cultural bias of this particular test. Was the vocabulary that was being tested relevant to the experiences of the children concerned, and also, was it context-embedded? We felt that some of it was 'context-embedded', but a great deal of it was probably beyond the cultural experiences of the bilingual children, testing fine nuances of the English language. For example, one word that the children were given was 'adjustable', and the correct picture was that of a belt!

The danger of such standardised tests is that it may be assumed from their results that bilingual learners are cognitively inferior to their monolingual peers. This in turn may mean that negative assumptions are made about the intellectual ability of bilingual learners so that they are given work that is cognitively less demanding. This type of testing can be particularly damaging when these tests are administered at the end of the primary school in order to stream pupils on entrance to secondary school. On the basis of such test results bilingual learners may well end up in the lower streams, which could affect their educational careers. All standardised tests that are given should be modified to ensure we are testing what the bilingual learner knows rather than what is outside their experience. This seems particularly important at the moment when so much emphasis is being placed on national testing. It also shows the importance of the Curriculum Related Assessment Sheets being used to give a fair 'teacher assessment' of a bilingual child's achievements, at a time when there is a move towards more teacher assessment.

Recording National Curriculum Levels in Science

A standard proforma has been used by a large consortium of schools in Hampshire for monitoring their pupils' achievements in science. These are the data collected throughout the children's lives in primary school, that will be passed to the secondary school at the end of Year 6. The level achieved by the pupil in each attainment target is recorded at the end of each term, and one would expect to see progression through the levels according to cognitive development. There is an area left blank for 'Further Information', and it is crucial that the teacher in the junior school gives a detailed account of what a developing bilingual learner can achieve in science, as levels cannot be achieved unless all strands of each statement are completed. Some of these strands put bilingual learners at a disadvantage.

For example, consider an Iraqi child (R) who arrived in school during the spring term of Year 6. R had followed programmes of study in her own country similar to those followed by her English peers. However, she had not encountered any practical work at all. She had learned English formally at her school in Iraq, but had had little experience of speaking and listening. and was still undergoing 'the silent phase' characteristic of newly-arrived bilingual learners. The class was undertaking a science AT1 experiment, and the task was 'Devise a way to make a model helicopter fly further'. This came about after work on seed dispersal. R was the only Arabic speaker in the school, and there were no Arabic-speaking adults.

I did not want to record failure for the attainment target (AT1) as I knew this did not reflect a true picture of R's understanding or capabilities. Once R had seen what the other pupils were doing, it was easy to explain to her what was expected, and she was able to complete the task. This she did by making several adaptations of the original model, testing them in collaboration with a monolingual peer, and recording her results.

Looking at the strand for AT1 in the National Curriculum, it was obvious that strand 1, 'Ask questions, predict and hypothesise' (planning), was not yet within R's capabilities in English. Predicting is difficult for developing bilingual pupils because it is language-embedded. The only way that R could have answered questions such as 'What do you think will happen?' would have been to work through her first language.

Strand 2 'Observe, measure and manipulate variables' (doing), was much easier for R to understand because it was a practical activity, and therefore context embedded. She obviously took cues from her peers, but was able to show understanding by employing her own ideas. She demonstrated her understanding of testing by dropping each model out of the window and measuring (a) the time it took to reach the ground, and (b) the distance from the building that it flew. She had therefore attained at least a level 3 in this strand. The original proforma gave no space to record this achievement except in the general section marked 'Further information'.

Strand 3, 'Interpret results and evaluate scientific evidence' (concluding), again proved to be very language-dependent. It was possible by using gestures and close questioning for R to indicate which model helicopter was most efficient, but without support in her mother tongue, it was not possible for her to say why or to match her observation with her prediction.

In this case, the proforma provided to record R's achievements in science was inappropriate, since it did not take account of bilingual pupils' capabilities and therefore could not portray a true picture of R's achievements when the Cummins model was taken into consideration. The secondary science teacher would therefore have had no knowledge of R's capabilities or past experiences, and this might have affected her expectations.

Section 11 Data Collection

The Home Office guidelines stipulate that bilingual pupils who are not achieving the national average in National Curriculum levels for English may be entitled to support from Section 11 teachers and bilingual assistants. Accordingly, schools when making a bid for Section 11 support, have to supply the levels for English ATs 1–5 for these pupils. Proformas are completed by schools, and information about pupils identified as underachievers (including their National Curriculum levels in English) is submitted to the Bilingual Learners Support Service. Unfortunately there are no guidelines for the collection of this information, except the general ones in the National Curriculum documents.

- For example, when assessing a bilingual child's level in speaking and listening (English AT1), we need to be aware of the following points:
- Is the subject matter culturally relevant to the pupil? e.g. The 'imaginative play' suggested as an activity at level 1 may be outside of the bilingual learner's experience if the teacher is not sensitive to the need of that child.
- Does the child have access to all non-verbal cues? i.e. Pictures, objects, gestures, teacher's facial expressions, blackboard etc.
- Is the group supportive of a bilingual pupil or dominated by monolingual pupils?
- Is the pupil able to respond non-verbally?
- Do the story books reflect a multicultural society, enabling all pupils to feel that they are valued members of the class?

- Is the pupil given a chance to hear good language models spoken before being asked to perform? e.g. By going last in a turn taking game.

In summary, is the Cummins model being considered? If the answer is no, then the level recorded for English AT1 may not have been a true record of a bilingual child's capabilities.

If a failure were to be recorded for the reading skills of a recently-arrived pupil, it would be useful to know if s/he were literate in his/her mother tongue. Many languages rely on the same skills being acquired by the child when decoding text (e.g. left-to right orientation and phonic analysis), and these skills do not need to be re-learned but simply transferred. A simple record of 'failure' in a box tells us nothing of a child's previous experiences, but a teacher needs to know of these before the learning process can continue. Older pupils achieving higher levels may still need support with the nuances of the English language, even though technically they are attaining a level similar to their monolingual peers. As with speaking and listening, a fair assessment of a bilingual learner's capabilities in reading is not possible unless a wide variety of reading material is available, with suitable subject matter to interest all children irrespective of their culture and age.

When assessing a bilingual pupil's level of achievement in writing (English AT3), we should also be aware of the context in which writing takes place in the classroom.

- Are pupils able to talk about their ideas in small groups before undertaking the task?
- Are the tasks staged so that the pupils are not confronted with a blank page on which to write 'a story'?
- If they are capable, are the pupils encouraged to write first drafts in their mother tongues so that their ideas may flow more freely?

Again the answers to these questions are interfaced with the Cummins model of good practice for bilingual learners.

Another consideration when assessing children's writing is the ESL developmental features that may be apparent. These do not correspond to the statements of attainment in the National Curriculum. Pupils may be assessed as being average writers for their age, but still be confusing tenses, using inappropriate prepositions, and omitting articles. Such children would benefit from the support that may be denied them if their needs are not brought to the attention of the support service.

Support services rely on the data submitted by schools in order to organise the deployment of their staff. The reliability of this information will be doubtful if the Cummins model was not considered when the assessments were taking place. As these assessments are ongoing, not the results of tests, we must employ appropriate methods of data collection, in order to ensure accurate information. Limited and therefore precious resources may be used inappropriately if incorrect or insufficient data are supplied, simply because there is no heading under which to record them.

Thus the assessment sheets and the model itself can contribute to the planning of teaching, to improved assessment. and to effective record keeping, provided that they are adapted to meet the particular needs of each classroom or school.

4 Differentiating the Secondary Curriculum

DERYN HALL

In this chapter I am proposing that the Cummins framework offers teachers a valuable tool for planning and differentiating the curriculum at Key Stages 3 and 4. It is a model which deserves to be more widely used and not only in the primary phase, because it helps us to consider the learning needs of three different groups of pupils in the classroom:

- bilingual pupils
- pupils with special educational needs
- very able pupils

In addition to its use as a model for formative assessment, it can help teachers think about providing contextual referents and better access for bilingual pupils; how to ensure that special education needs (as defined in the 1993 Education Act) are met; and how to meet the needs of able pupils in terms of greater cognitive demand, thus enhancing academic achievement for all pupils.

Defining Differentiation

Differentiation has become one of the educational buzz words of the 1990's. It is, as Visser (1993a) points out, 'used by many, understood by some and put fully into practice by a few'. As it is one of the aspects of classroom teaching which will receive attention in OFSTED inspections, it is essential that teachers are helped to a clearer understanding of differentiation as a process in their planning and teaching.

One of the earliest references to differentiation was made in an H.M.I. Discussion Paper (1978) which observed that '. . . many of the examples seen failed to provide differentiation, confused pace of work with level of work by simply asking more able pupils to do more of the same in the available time and did not offer problem solving opportunities'. In the period since 1978 many different views have been put forward on how differentiation is best defined.

In practice, differentiation is the process whereby curriculum aims, teaching and assessment methods, resources and tasks are planned by teachers to take account of individual pupil need. Ann Robson (1991) has defined these needs as being along three different dimensions. These are (a) the particular learning styles and needs of individual pupils, (b) the requirements of the learning task, and (c) the context of the situation where the learning will take place. So conversely, differentiation could be seen as teachers using information about pupils' needs and knowledge about task demands and contexts to plan an appropriate curriculum. In a model offered by King (1989) all these dimensions are included in a 'Differentiation Menu'.

Other models have tried to suggest that there are two main ways of differentiating learning activities, by task and by outcome. Differentiating by task requires the teacher to develop activities which help pupils achieve the lesson objectives. The idea is that the teacher should set different tasks within a common area of study. Factors affecting the difficulty of a task include pupils' familiarity with the concepts and language used; familiarity with the materials and resources used; and the extent to which models, prompts and concrete referents are made available by the teacher. Differentiation by outcome involves setting a common task for the class. The assumption is that pupils' learning outcomes will be varied according to their individual aptitudes and interests. In this case it is important that every pupil is clear what the task requires but more open ended tasks allowing for pupil negotiation about their responses are probably the most effective. Well planned and lively stimuli will motivate pupils to work to their full potential. More able pupils could be expected to use more difficult concepts, carry out more complex and advanced operations and express themselves in more sophisticated vocabulary. Such models and definitions have served to focus attention on the mainstream learning environment and appropriate access for bilingual and special needs pupils.

Differentiation then, can be interpreted in various ways, but broadly it is seen as a concern to meet the learning needs of all pupils within mainstream classes. Sometimes this has meant schools/teachers responding to differences solely in terms of pupils' cognitive ability. Frequently the solution to this is seen in terms of 'setting', 'banding' or streaming by ability. For pupils whose first language is other than English there are equal opportunity issues of language access. They may be pupils with considerable cognitive ability who need help to demonstrate mastery of concepts in a second language. However they are unlikely to be placed with others of their own ability because of their limited command of English.

Other solutions to differentiating the curriculum have meant differing aims, courses or tasks; different content, pace, scope or depth of study; even a consideration of the amount of reinforcement required by individual pupils within a class group. A DES (1989) definition centred on these individual differences among pupils and how these can be accommodated. It stated that schools should provide an 'entitlement curriculum' for all pupils which should have 'breadth, balance, relevance, progression, continuity and differentiation'. In order to make better sense and meaning out of this educational jargon Visser (1993a) put these words into a coherent sentence:

> All pupils are entitled to a broad, balanced curriculum; delivered in a relevant and differentiated manner enabling progression and continuity to be experienced.

From this it is much clearer to see that differentiation is a process whereby teachers try to ensure their pupils' progress through the curriculum by selecting appropriate teaching methods and materials to match individual pupils' learning strategies within a group teaching situation as far as possible. The concept of group is an important one as this represents the reality of most class teaching.

An expectation that schools might move towards the sort of differentiation associated with 'individual learning programmes' for all is an unrealistic one. Firstly, the challenge for the teacher in terms of numbers of pupils and time would make its management impossible even if it were desirable. Secondly, individualised programmes of work are rarely sufficiently differentiated in terms of language, cognition or preferred learning styles. Thirdly, pupils working alone easily become demotivated, understimulated and bored. The lack of opportunity to work with others who are more or less able or simply those who think differently from oneself would seem to me undesirable on social grounds alone.

Differentiation: A Process

Differentiation should ensure that the curriculum offered is both appropriate and motivating for all pupils, and thus the process also has a role to play in sustaining positive pupil behaviour at school. It means that teachers are required to reflect and focus on the learning process. In the past couple of years we have seen an over-emphasis on curriculum content as schools have struggled to come to terms with weighty National Curriculum documentation. Educational debate has centred on testing and content to the detriment of a real consideration of methodology and the ways in which pupils best learn. We need a speedy return to some of the earlier research and good practice in terms of the 'how' and not just the 'what' of teaching if we are to rescue the baby from drowning in the bath water! By taking a model of curriculum as one which consists of an equal emphasis on its component parts of methodology, organisation and content we might be helped towards a better balanced classroom offer.

An emphasis on pupil diversity seen in terms of age, aptitude or ability and resolved by setting or banding does not actually give pupils more homogeneity of attitudes, beliefs or values; in fact, it could be said to enhance difference. Teachers need to develop some understanding of individual pupil's learning strategies and whether some of these are more efficient than others for the acquisition of particular skills. Teaching methodology needs to be closely matched to what we know from research about these observed strategies. One of the most important aims of differentiation should be to help pupils take an increasingly greater responsibility for their own learning.

It is possible that the Cummins matrix is an important tool simply because it offers us a way of thinking about and a better awareness of the learning needs of these pupils in planning curriculum. The Cummins matrix may offer us a helpful way of thinking about the learning needs of these pupils so that they can operate more autonomously and take such responsibility. That issue is discussed in more detail in the final section of this chapter.

Principles of Good Practice for Bilingual Children

Many of the recent initiatives in education come together in the search for good practice in the teaching of bilingual children within the mainstream classroom and there is a wide consensus in this country as to what constitutes this. Recent work on Partnership Teaching (Bourne and McPake 1991), the National Oracy Project (1993), active teaching and learning and collaborative and group work in the classroom all contribute to our knowledge of a methodology that is highly relevant in ensuring curricular access for bilingual pupils. It is as follows:

Working in partnership

It is now standard practice in this country to try to support pupils learning English as a Second Language within the mainstream classroom as part of normal lessons. In the past it was believed that bilingual pupils learning English needed special teaching methods and materials not necessarily relevant or appropriate to other pupils. More recently, linguists and educationalists have recognised that the teaching methodologies developed as a response to mixed ability classes are also those that are relevant and appropriate for bilingual learners.

Oracy: The role of talk in classrooms

The organisation of the classroom to enable pupils to work in groups cannot be emphasised enough. This is an essential part of the active learning strategies encouraged by The National Oracy Project (1987–1993) and greatly benefits bilingual pupils in a number of ways. Talk is the vital key to language acquisition.

Use of mother tongue in the classroom

For bilingual learners the opportunity to use their first language is a way of confirming language and meaning and the conceptualisation of complex issues will be enhanced. Pupils must be encouraged to use their first languages in the classroom but they will be more prepared to support their learning and understanding in this way if their community language has a high status at school. For this reason pupils' home languages and experiences must be not only valued and recognised but developed and utilised.

Active and collaborative learning in small groups

Pupils working cooperatively on tasks in groups share skills and ideas and work together to support each other. This is important in developing a supportive classroom atmosphere where pupils can learn to give and receive help from each other independently of the teacher. Each pupil in every group helps to formulate and expand ideas, and during the process of problem solving, pupils are using skills of negotiating, prioritising, investigating, drafting, sequencing, matching. Typical exchanges might include practising language structures such as questioning, reflecting, suggesting, prediction and hypothesis.

The Cummins Model

What then does the Cummins model have to offer us in attempting to implement this good practice for bilingual pupils in secondary classrooms within the framework of the National Curriculum? This account will answer that question by describing developments undertaken in the East London borough of Tower Hamlets where over sixty per cent of the school population overall are bilingual. The challenges of bilingualism for teachers have been as follows:

- raising teacher expectation;
- raising educational achievement;
- accessing bilingual pupils to National Curriculum;
- early identification of bilingual pupils who may have learning difficulties;

It seems possible that the multi-dimensional Cummins framework is the one theoretical model for differentiation which can address all these issues.

The contributors to the set of working papers in Frederickson and Cline (1990) based on Cummins' model were largely educational psychologists who were seeking methods of curriculum related assessment which would be of particular relevance in assessing bilingual pupils whose learning was causing [their monolingual teachers] concern. Several uses were suggested for the Cummins framework at this stage. In addition to its use for assessment purposes a tentative idea was proposed that it may have potential as a tool for topic planning and 'for differentiating classroom tasks'. However, the National Curriculum was in its early days, and there were some problems in trying to apply the framework to it. Examples given were only for Key Stage 1 and the primary curriculum. The challenge which I will discuss here was to see if the model had any validity for use by teachers in planning and differentiating the curriculum in secondary schools.

How can we ensure that bilingual pupils are accessed into the curriculum and that they are making progress in terms of achievement? We need to satisfy ourselves that we are making increasing cognitive demands whilst providing concrete referents and comprehensible contexts in terms of both content and process. For teachers in Tower Hamlets secondary schools, the challenge is to move bilingual pupils from context embedded conversation to context reduced discussion as efficiently as possible to increase their chance of good academic qualifications (see Figure 4.1). Without these, their chances of employment in the local area are drastically reduced.

The Framework in Use

In discussing and planning with the Cummins model I have decided that the lower right hand quadrant should really remain blank. To me it seems self evident that if tasks or lesson content were to be 'cognitively undemanding and context reduced' pupils should not be wasting their time

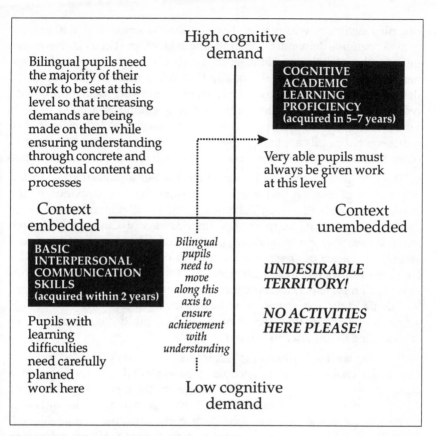

Figure 4.1 The Cummins matrix

doing them! Both primary and secondary teachers can always think of examples of this in practice with little difficulty, however. These activities are usually described as something like 'mindlessly colouring in' or 'tearing up coloured tissue paper into little bits and sticking them back together on another piece of paper' as one primary teacher vividly described it! For secondary teachers the irrelevant task is inevitably 'copying writing off the board when they [bilingual pupils] haven't got a clue what it's about or why they are copying it.' Inevitably these activities are not regarded as good practice for any pupil.

It is interesting that teachers using the model feel that it is the top left hand quadrant which is the most demanding for teachers. Because of the work and size of the Language Achievement Project in the East End of London (Section 11 funded from 1992) most teachers felt confident in planning activities which were heavily context embedded without too great a cognitive demand. Given first language support in their classrooms most teachers felt they could meet the needs of bilingual pupils who were new to English at this level. Equally they felt confident that they could design tasks and activities which were cognitively demanding with reduced context for the more able pupils operating at a good level of English language competence. The real challenge was felt to be that of ensuring that pupils are being cognitively stretched whilst continuing to embed the learning in sufficient context to acquire more complex concepts.

There is general concern in our schools about a plateau effect in the acquisition of English and a need to ensure that the demands of the curriculum are high whilst acknowledging the continued necessity of providing contextual support. The implications of Cummins' research make it clear that many bilingual pupils need several years (from 5 to 7 years) experience of classroom learning in order to acquire the kind of language proficiency to achieve good grades within the demands of our examination system. If teachers can ensure that they are not making tasks less demanding and therefore reducing their expectations of a child's academic potential, they can then plead 'not guilty 'to accusations of contributing to 'underachievement'.

Working with teachers on the Cummins Matrix has presented me with two major challenges. Firstly, could it be extended into the secondary curriculum or was the model only suitable for the more integrated topic approach of a primary classroom? I will provide two examples of how a successful extension into the secondary curriculum has been achieved. Secondly, would the model be useful both for the more affective domains of the curriculum such as English and Humanities and for the more conceptual areas such as Maths and Science?

'Romeo and Juliet' (English KS3)

These materials were initially developed by Claudine Field in partnership with Stuart Scott as resources for distribution through the Collaborative Learning Project which serves as a resources 'swapshop' for teachers. They have subsequently been trialled and developed further, and a similar methodology has been applied in making other difficult texts accessible. The pack of introductory materials based on Romeo and Juliet supports the teaching of Shakespeare at Key Stage 3 (Field, 1993). It suggests activities for group work on the story, the prologue, the characters, key speeches/Shakespeare's language, and the theme of 'responsibility'. It is intended as an introduction to the play and is not intended to supplant the other work which will be planned by English teachers in the study of a Shakespeare text. Some of the activities are available in differentiated forms. For example, the Character cards are available in standard, simplified, Bengali and Turkish versions. The prologue is available for a sequencing exercise as couplets in the original language, in simple modern English and as a set of pictorial clues. The activities are not intended to be worked through in any particular sequence but offer ideas for different group activities.

Story

The activity most suitable for introducing the story prior to reading the text is 'Invent your own Romeo and Juliet'. Using the pictures provided, the pupils work in groups to make up their own story based around the pictures. They then reassemble them in poster form and produce captions to explain what happens in their story. Blank boxes are provided for extra drawings if necessary. Each group then tells their story to the rest of the class. A 'key words' sheet is provided to support those pupils with less experience in English. These can also be used to match the illustrations to make posters. All these activities belong in the lower left hand quadrant as they are low demand tasks well supported by the visual clues. A story 'summary', and a sequenced version of it, is also provided to match with the pictures when Shakespeare's version is introduced.

Prologue

Shakespeare's prologue is available as a sequencing exercise using language from the text. Without contextual support this is a highly cognitively demanding task. A glossary of more difficult words would give some additional support to bilingual pupils. In addition a modern English version is included which can be matched to Shakespeare's language at a lesser level of cognitive demand. Again, picture 'clues' are given to provide contextual support for each couplet so it is possible for all pupils to have access to the prologue content. (See Appendix.) The 'real' story of Romeo and Juliet can now be introduced.

Able pupils should be able to negotiate the sequencing of the story from the summary without the visual prompts which provide a visual access to the English. Copies of the play as a standard class text should be made available, and the abbreviated text and prose versions of Leon Garfield also provide a useful resource for accessing the story. [The latter version is also available in an abbreviated form.]

Characters

The activity based on the main characters of the play is an oracy exercise based on the theory that having to present facts or knowledge verbally to others is one of the best ways to reinforce learning. Even quite abstract concepts can be successfully acquired by this method. I have used it successfully with bilingual year 7 students to learn such terms as 'cytoplasm' and 'chlorophyll' in cell biology. Again, character cards are provided at two levels of reading difficulty. An example of a standard character card in the simplest version has the following text: 'Juliet is fourteen years old . . . She is in love with Romeo.' Translated versions are available in Bengali and Turkish. Blank cards are provided for a second activity and these could be used by very able students to research a character from the text, to create their own 'character reference'. Alternatively they might be given act and scene references to find information on more minor characters.

The active learning from this activity occurs from oral work in pairs and then fours. Pupils spend two minutes reading the information about their character on their card. Then they tell their partner about that character as if they were that person. Careful listening is required during the minute allowed for each person to do this as pupils then have to introduce each other (in role) to the other pair. By the end of this ten minute activity pupils will have found out some information on four characters in the play. Pupils can add their own information on the characters from any other sources. The second activity is a card game for groups of 4 to 8 pupils who will each be given one of the character cards. The 40 blank cards can be used by the pupils themselves to devise five questions about each other in role as one of Shakespeare's eight characters which are drawn in turn from a central stack. Pupils can devise their own rules of play and can assess the value of their questions in an evaluation and report back.

A Connect Four game is also offered at two levels of difficulty. The first uses simple statements about the characters while the second uses direct quotations by the characters from the text. Follow on work requires pupils to fill in the information they have from the game onto a chart and to add to it any additional information they can find about each of the eight characters.

Key speeches/Shakespearean language

This activity encourages pupils to use the text in the context of a drama activity. This allows them the opportunity to increase their reading of Shakespearean language and to make their own notes from the text. Key speeches can be learnt by heart whilst working cooperatively to produce a short piece of drama. Pupils are given a brief summary of one act of the play together with selected speeches which they must produce as a five minute dramatic presentation. Tape recorders can be used to rehearse speeches, and the final presentation could be videoed. The pupils will need access to the text to find out what happens in between the given speeches and to write a brief summary of the story to link the scene together. The pupils then decide how to present their act dividing the work so that all group members have a role to play. As long as they include the given speeches, they can choose to act the whole scene in modern English or to use a narrator to set the action between key speeches or present a tableau with commentary and mime.

A simpler additional activity which could be given as a homework activity to reinforce individual understanding of Shakespearean language is a 'Quote Quest' task of matching quotations from the text to statements.

Theme of responsibility

This activity can be used as an introduction to a piece of extended oral or written work and is a group activity based on a 'diamond mine' model for group negotiation and discussion. Pupils are presented with ten possible sources of 'blame' for the tragedy and are asked to prioritise a hierarchy noting down additional reasons for their agreed choice. This can be reported back to the class and followed up as a debate or courtroom tribunal with pupils in role giving evidence or as a discursive or critical essay. At this level the activity is cognitively highly demanding and context reduced.

Plotting the activities

In discussion with Field who had trialled the original material in schools in Hackney and Tower Hamlets, the activities were drafted onto the Cummin's matrix (see Figure 4.2). For all these activities it is assumed that the pupils will be organised into groups. It is also envisaged that two teachers, one from the English Department with one support teacher, will work together in a collaborative way over the course of several lessons for this unit of work. The activities assume no prior knowledge of the play or the plot but neither will prior knowledge detract from the value of the activities in their own right.

High cognitive
demand

prologue
using pictorial clues to match and
sequence couplets from prologue

character
'2 minute autobiographies' using
cards

text
'quote quest': matching quotations
to statements about character

prologue
modern English version matched
to text

prologue
modern English version matched
with story

prologue
sequencing prologue couplets
(without clues)

character
research using blank cards/
devise quiz game using
information from text

text
'filling the gaps' using speeches
from key scenes and full text to
research before and after

theme
'who was to blame?' prepare
debate for tribunal or discursive
essay

Context
embedded

Context
unembedded

character
'connect four': statement about
character

story
'summary' matched with
sequenced pictures

story
'invent your own Romeo and
Juliet' sequencing pictures and
telling story from them

story
pictures and 'key words' making
posters for wall display using key
words

Romeo & Juliet
English KS3

Texts to be made available
to pupils:
– standard school text
– abbreviated text
– prose version
– abbreviated prose text

(Leon Garfield texts)
Animated Shakespeare
films also useful

Low cognitive
demand

Figure 4.2 The Romeo and Juliet activities shown as a Cummins matrix

Figure 4.2 demonstrates one way in which these activities might be placed onto a Cummins matrix. Because of the very individual ways in which teachers will use the same materials and the different methods and purposes to which they can be utilised, this is, of course, a subject for debate. The great strength of collaborative working is the level of this debate and the questioning which takes place in the planning process. Used as a workshop activity, this discussion about cognitive demand and access for pupils with little English spurs teachers into creative ideas for using the materials to meet the demands of their particular pupil group. Many teachers who have used these materials have adapted and added ideas of their own. Hopefully the plotting of some of these materials onto a Cummins matrix will encourage teachers to use and develop a similar methodology in planning a differentiated curriculum. The matrix could also be used to assess the pupils' level of work with the materials and to plan appropriate further support or extension activities within further English programmes of study.

'Adaptation' (Science KS3)

As a further demonstration that the model can be used as a tool for differentiation in different areas of the curriculum, I include a description of some thinking about the conceptually difficult topic of adaptation which is part of Key Stage 3 AT2 'Life and Living Processes' (see Figure 4.3). Under 'Living things in their environment: 6a adaptation', the revised National Curriculum for Science suggests that pupils should be taught 'how organisms are adapted to survive daily and seasonal changes in their habitats'. This work is often studied in Year 7 classes and includes such topics as 'properties of living things'; classification using keys; predator/prey; feeding relationships; competition, abundance and distribution. Frequently, because of the pressure of the amount of content which must be covered in each science unit, only one double lesson and a homework are allocated to the topic of adaptation. It is a topic which is difficult to access to bilingual pupils and which seems thinly, if at all, covered in the standard textbooks. The following method has been successfully used by language support teachers at one local school. It assumes that definitions of the technical vocabulary such as 'habitat' and 'living things' have been previously taught.

Pupils are organised into groups for the introductory activity – the Habitat Game. Each group is given an A3 photocopied illustration (or photograph) of one habitat. These can include rainforest, prairie, desert, polar region, ocean/coral reef, farmyard, freshwater pond/river. Each

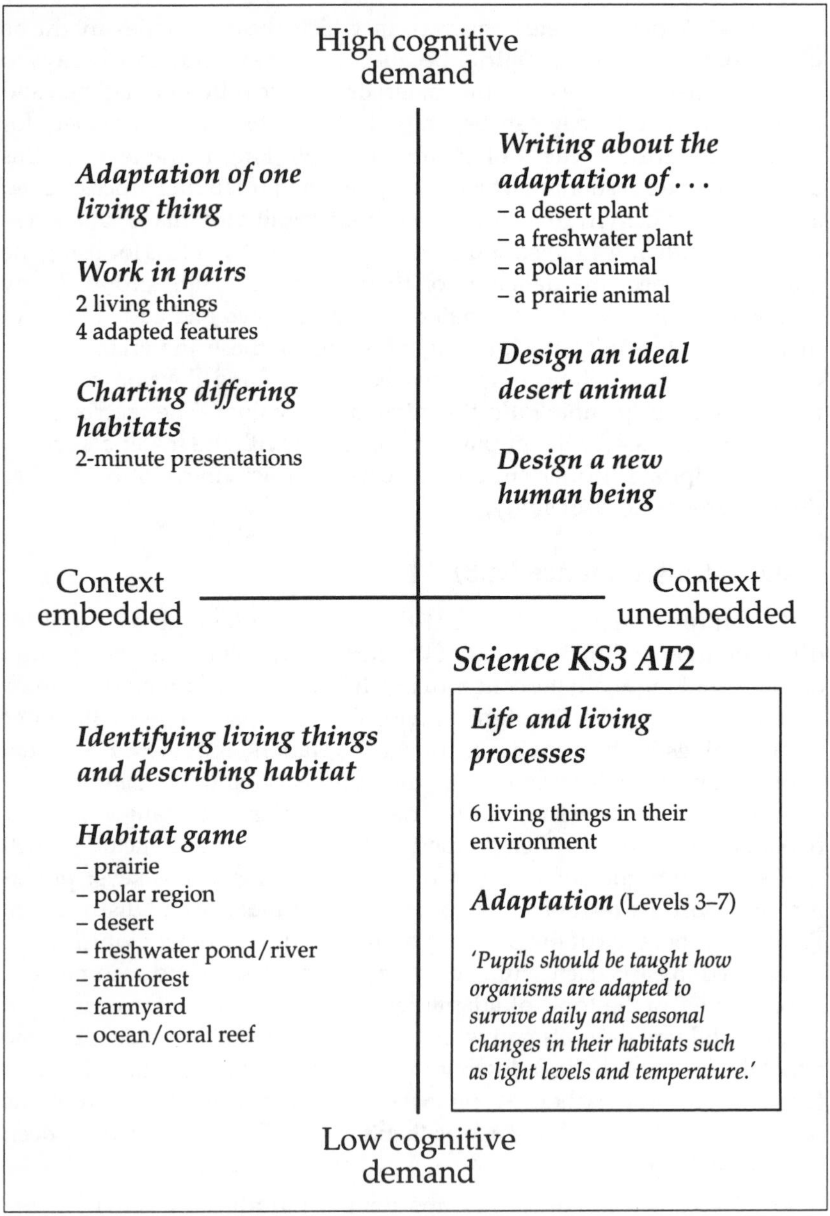

High cognitive
demand

*Adaptation of one
living thing*

Work in pairs
2 living things
4 adapted features

*Charting differing
habitats*
2-minute presentations

*Writing about the
adaptation of . . .*
– a desert plant
– a freshwater plant
– a polar animal
– a prairie animal

*Design an ideal
desert animal*

*Design a new
human being*

Context
embedded

Context
unembedded

Science KS3 AT2

*Identifying living things
and describing habitat*

Habitat game
– prairie
– polar region
– desert
– freshwater pond/river
– rainforest
– farmyard
– ocean/coral reef

*Life and living
processes*

6 living things in their
environment

Adaptation (Levels 3–7)

*'Pupils should be taught how
organisms are adapted to
survive daily and seasonal
changes in their habitats such
as light levels and temperature.'*

Low cognitive
demand

Figure 4.3 The Adaptation activities shown as a Cummins matrix

group is also given an envelope containing ten small pictures of different plants/animals. They have to discuss which of the living things belongs in 'their' habitat and place them on the picture. They then need to decide what other living things, plant and animal, might belong in their habitat and act as 'negotiators' in turn to arrange swaps by visiting other groups. Each group negotiator can only negotiate with one habitat group at a time and each group can only swap one living thing per visit. The aim is to collect all ten cards for your own habitat. Each group then matches labels to the living things in their habitats and writes some sentences to describe the habitat on a chart. This might include some consideration under headings of climate and vegetation, food sources and predators. Follow on work from this could involve a two minute oral presentation about the living things in each habitat with hypotheses as to how/why the living things are well adapted to live in each. Groups then visit other habitats to note down on a chart features of each and the names of the living things found there.

Pupils can then work in pairs from additional information cards, choosing two living things from different habitats and listing four ways in which each is well adapted to its environment. Home work or extension tasks might include any of the following. All pupils should be able to write about the adaptation of one living thing to its environment using vocabulary and notes from the lesson. More able pupils can write about the adaptation of at least one of each of – a desert plant, a polar animal, a fresh water plant, or a prairie animal. They may draw on the information provided in library/topic books. Some pupils might attempt to design an ideal desert animal with features which are well adapted to the habitat by a critical analysis of information gleaned from topic books about deserts. Very able pupils might attempt a task of designing a new human being to survive the difficulties likely to face the human race in the future with notes which give reasons for the choice of features. This would require a critical evaluation of environmental evidence and a development of ideas and hypotheses.

Although the activities require some time and effort initially in collecting of information, photocopying, cutting and pasting, the materials can then be used for all groups in the year and will be available in subsequent years to support this topic. Where schools have support teachers for language or learning, there is often a resource development brief as part of the job description. As the National Curriculum now requires the repetition of units of work in terms of curriculum content for each successive year group, it is well worth the initial effort put in to plan these collaborative and differentiated activities which attempt to provide access for the diverse range of pupils in our classrooms.

generalises

compares and *contrasts*

summarises

plans

classifies by known criteria

transforms, personalises given information

recalls and *reviews*

seeks solutions to problems

argues a case using evidence persuasively

identifies criteria, develops and *sustains* ideas

justifies opinion or judgement

evaluates critically

interprets evidence, makes deductions

forms hypotheses, asks further questions for investigation

predicts results

applies principles to new situation

analyses, suggests solution and tests

$\left(\textit{Cognitive processes}\right)$

reading to find specific information

– *identifies*

– *names*

– *matches*

– *retells*

transfers information from one medium to another

applies known procedures

describes observations

sequences

narrates with sense of beginning, middle, end

parrots: repeats utterances of adult or peer

copies: reproduces information from board or texts

Figure 4.4 Mapping cognitive processes

Mapping Cognitive Processes

Figure 4.4 shows an attempt to map some of the more common classroom cognitive processes onto the Cummins matrix. This has not been made subject specific and it does not claim to include all possible processes which pupils may be engaged in during their secondary schooling. However it is useful to acknowledge the range of these and for teachers to be aware of how they fit within the framework when thinking about how to 'cater appropriately for the learning of pupils with differing abilities and interests and ensure the full participation of all' (OFSTED, 1993).

In the lower right hand quadrant are copying responses for both speaking and writing which require little or no thinking or use of memory. In the lower left hand quadrant are responses to tasks in which the pupil is required to observe, identify, name, describe or sequence things which are present. At this stage the pupil is not required to transform the material in any way. At this level the pupil may be asked to retell something just actively experienced or to transfer the same information from one medium to another.

Moving up the cognitive demand axis are the next level of activities which are still reliant on good contextual first hand experience. Here the pupil can plan by known criteria, compare and contrast, summarise, generalise, recall, classify, seek solutions to problems and discuss cause and effect. The pupil is required to pull information and rules together, to explain the cause of an event, and eventually learns to transform information, construct rules and formulate generalisations.

The higher order skills of the top right hand quadrant will be familiar to teachers as commensurate with higher level descriptors of the recent draft proposals of SCAA (School Curriculum and Assessment Authority). Here pupils can be expected to form and test hypotheses, predict results, apply principles to new problems, analyse, develop and sustain ideas, suggest alternatives, use and add to given information, identify criteria, interpret evidence and make deductions. They can argue a case persuasively using evidence to support their stance and justify their opinion or judgement critically.

Purists will argue that these statements are fairly general abstractions which, separated from their actual contexts, can be open to some debate. Working with a group of teachers on this exercise elicits cries of 'it all depends on the task'. For some it may only serve to provide a useful forum for debate, but for others it could be a tool to inform and benefit classroom practice.

It is probable that the model does not stand up to tight academic scrutiny in many ways, and there are certainly areas of debate where it is used as a suggested curriculum planning tool with groups of teachers. There is some justifiable argument as to whether context can be sufficiently separated from cognitive content. However, this does not detract from the model's usefulness as a tool. Furthermore, this usefulness does not seem contentious among practising teachers who are natural sceptics! It has not been rejected outright by any of the primary or secondary groups with whom I have worked. The level of debate generated in the process of collaborative planning during the workshops means that teachers are considerably raising their own awareness of the needs of several groups of pupils. The model also seems to have great 'street credibility'; an important factor for overstretched members of the teaching profession who need new ideas like a hole in the head after the recent rapid changes at local and national level!

The sheer simplicity of the matrix is a major advantage. It seems to make explicit certain pupil needs without the expectation that teachers will necessarily have time to refer to the literature. It also seems to make a fairly immediate sense which serves to confirm teachers' intuitive knowledge of individual differences within the classroom. An understanding of the dimensions of the model can serve to allay fears of OFSTED inspections by an increased awareness of the need for differentiated planning and classroom activities. Although there are complaints about the jargon used to describe the dimensions of the model (and we generally make it worse in attempting to come up with alternatives!) the important considerations it carries are simple, accessible and relevant. Few teachers have met the model previously, except for some who have attended further training courses in the teaching of English as a Second Language. Yet the model's ability to be worked in terms of the demands of National Curriculum and the need to differentiate it within classrooms are considerable bonuses. For these reasons alone it is worth more serious consideration by practising teachers and teacher trainers.

Appendix: Examples from the 'Romeo and Juliet' Materials

Romeo and Juliet

Each of these pictures illustrates two lines of the Prologue.
Use them to help put the mixed up lines of the Prologue into the right order.

Romeo and Juliet   The Prologue

Two equally rich and important families live in Verona, where our play is set.

They hate each other because of an old argument. Now the argument has begun again and people get hurt in the fighting.

The two families have two children who are cursed with bad luck. They fall in love with each other, and kill themselves.

The deaths of their children ends the fighting between the two sets of parents.

The tragic bad luck of the lovers, and the fighting between their parents,

(which only their children's deaths could end), is now the subject of our play.

So if you listen carefully to our play, you will find out exactly what happened.

Romeo and Juliet

*This is the prologue of the play 'Romeo and Juliet'. The sequence of the lines has been muddled up. **Your task** is to rearrange them so that they make sense.*

From ancient grudge break to new mutiny,
Where civil blood makes civil hands unclean.

Whose misadventured piteous overthrows
Doth with their death bury their parents' strife.

Two households, both alike in dignity,
In fair Verona (where we lay our scene),

From forth the fatal loins of these two foes
A pair of star-crossed lovers take their life;

The which if you with patient ears attend,
What here shall miss, our toil shall strive to mend.

Which but their children's end nought could remove,
Is now the two hours' traffic of our stage;

The fearful passage of their death-marked love,
And the continuance of their parents' rage,

References and further reading

Alexander, R. *et al.* (1992) ['Three Wise Men Report'] *The Education of Very Able Children in Maintained Schools.* London: HMI.

Barnes, D. (1989) *Active Learning.* University of Leeds.

— (1992) The role of talk in learning. In K. Norman (ed.) *Thinking Voices.* London: Hodder and Stoughton.

Barthorpe, T. and Visser, J. (1991) *Differentiation: Your Responsibility.* Stafford: NASEN.

Bennett, N. and Barnes, D. (1992) *Managing Classroom Groups.* Simon and Schuster.

Bourne, J. and McPake, J.(1991) *Partnership Teaching.* London: NFER/DES for HMSO.

Brandes, D. and Ginnis, P. (1986) *A Guide to Student Centred Learning.* Oxford: Basil Blackwell.

Cline, T. and Frederickson, N. (1991) *Bilingual Pupils and the National Curriculum.* London: University College.

CRE (1986) *The Teaching of English as a Second Language: The Report of a Formal Investigation in Calderdale LEA.* London: Commission for Racial Equality.

DES (1985) [The Swann Report] *Education for All: The Report of the Committee of Enquiry into the Education of Children from Ethnic Minorities.* London: HMSO.

— (1989) *The National Curriculum: From Policy To Practice.* London: DES/HMSO.

— (1989) *National Curriculum Working Group. English for ages 5–16.* DES/Welsh Office.

Field, C. (1993) *Collaborative Learning Project: Romeo and Juliet.* (These materials are available by post from: Language Support Service, P.D.C., English Street, Mile End, London E3 4TA, Tel 0171 981 0183.)

Frederickson, N. and Cline, T. (1990) *Curriculum Related Assessment with Bilingual Children.* London: University College.

HMI (1978) *Matters for Discussion 6: Mixed Ability Work in Comprehensive Schools.* London: HMSO.

— (1986) *A Survey of the Teaching of English as a Second Language in Six LEAs.* London: DES.

— (1990) *Aspects of Primary Education: The Teaching and Learning of Language and Literacy.* London: HMSO.

Jenkin, F. (1989) *Making Small Groups Work.* Exeter: Pergamon Educational Products.

King, V. (1989) Differentiation is the key. *Language and Learning 3.*

Lunzer, E. and Gardner, K. (eds) (1979) *The Effective Use of Reading.* London: Heinemann.

Lunzer, E., Gardner, K., Davis, F. and Greene, T. (1984) *Learning from the Written Word.* Edinburgh: Oliver and Boyd.

National Oracy Project (1993) In G. Baddeley (ed.) *Learning Together Through Talk KS1&2*; and H. Kemeny (ed.) *Learning Together Through Talk KS3&4.* London: Hodder and Stoughton.

OFSTED (1993) *Handbook for the Inspection of Schools.* London: HMSO.

Peters, M. (ed.) (1992) Differentiation. *British Journal of Special Education* 19 (1).

Reid, J., Forrestal, P. and Cook, J. (1989) *Small Group Learning in the Classroom.* Chalk Face Press.

Robson, A. (1991) Differentiation for bilingual pupils in the National Curriculum. In T. Cline and F. Frederickson (eds) *Bilingual Pupils and The National Curriculum.*

London: University College.

Sheffield City Polytechnic [Sheffield Hallam University] Centre for Science Education. (1992) *Active Teaching and Learning Approaches in Science*. London: Collins Educational.

Spillman, J. (1991) Decoding 'differentiation'. *Special Children*, January 1991

Stradling, R. and Saunders, L. (1991) *Differentiation in Action: A Whole School Approach*. London: HMSO.

Visser, J. (1993a) *Differentiation: Making It Work*. Stafford: NASEN.

— (1993b) A broad, balanced, relevant and differentiated curriculum. In J. Visser G. Upton (eds) *Special Education in Britain after Warnock*. London: David Fulton.

Wilkinson, A., Davies, A. and Atkinson, D. (1965) *Spoken English*. University of Birmingham.

Section 3:
Support for Children with Special Educational Needs

Introduction

Jim Cummins first applied his model to issues in special education ten years ago (Cummins, 1984). This section comprises two chapters which provide quite different illustrations of the value of the framework in work with children with special educational needs. In Chapter 5 Usha Rogers and Alan Pratten discuss work with bilingual children who present as experiencing learning difficulties in mainstream schools. They have used the Cummins framework as a decision making aid. In Chapter 6 Ann Robson describes how the framework can be adapted for work with children with hearing impairment. Separate editorial introductions are provided for each chapter.

5 The Cummins Framework as a Decision Making Aid for Special Education Professionals Working with Bilingual Children

USHA ROGERS AND ALAN R. PRATTEN

Editorial Introduction

This chapter provides a way of examining a question of fundamental importance to special education professionals working with bilingual children for whom the language of instruction is not their preferred language. When does poor learning performance indicate a special educational need and when does it indicate a need for further support in learning the language of instruction (Cline & Frederickson, 1991)? This decision between the identification of learning needs and language needs is often fraught with difficult political and ethical considerations. If the special education professional mistakenly decides that a child has a learning need then the child may be provided with insufficiently challenging learning experiences and be subject to inappropriately low expectations. What is more, the sharp demarcation and poor liaison which sometimes exists between learning and language support services means that the language support (which is what the child actually needs) will probably cease and responsibility for their support will be transferred to the learning support services. This is likely to produce a self fulfilling prophesy unless the child is particularly resilient or their teachers particularly perceptive. Decision errors of this type may also lay the special education professional open to charges of racism or of employing culturally biased assessment procedures.

However, difficulties also are created by mistaken decisions that a child has a language rather than a learning need. In this case the child is likely to receive a language support programme to which they cannot respond because its pace is too fast and it is structured in learning steps which are too large. In subsequent assessment therefore they will continue to present as having language needs, so it may be several years before it is finally recognised that their difficulties with learning language are not responsible for their slow academic progress but that problems in both areas reflect general learning difficulties.

Maintaining the 'language difficulties' hypothesis until the evidence for 'learning difficulties' becomes overwhelming avoids the political pitfalls for professionals outlined above. However, it presents serious ethical problems in that the children concerned are deprived, sometimes for a number of years, of the special learning support which they need. This is likely to have serious consequences – for the children's future learning progress and for their self esteem. It may also have consequences for their special educational placement: support required at an early stage is more likely to be provided in an integrated mainstream programme, whereas waiting until the child's needs are obviously desperate would increase the likelihood of a segregated special school placement.

The cost of errors in decision making is so great that special education professionals must take all possible steps to minimise the risk of their occurrence. This chapter describes the approach adopted by the Educational Psychology Service in one English county. The approach is of interest in two major respects – first, and of central importance to the theme of this book, is the way in which the Cummins framework is used as an aid to decision making – in structuring the diverse assessment information collected and in aiding its analysis and interpretation. Essentially the approach involves using the Cummins framework to map the tasks on which the children can succeed and those which they are unable to do. For the latter further assessment involves increasing the level of contextual support as a first step. This may entail increasing non–verbal cues such as those gained from demonstration to support the verbal message. Learning experiences may also be contextually embedded by supplementing the language of tuition with explanation or examples in the child's preferred language. This strategy requires the involvement of adults who speak the child's preferred language and the second feature of interest in the approach described in this chapter is the way in which educational psychologists and bilingual support teachers work together, so integrating the learning and language expertise which is so often uncoordinated.

Figures 5.1 and 5.2 provide schematic snapshots of the kinds of profiles which may be interpreted as indicating learning and language needs respectively.

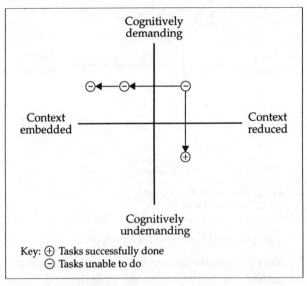

Figure 5.1 A child with learning needs

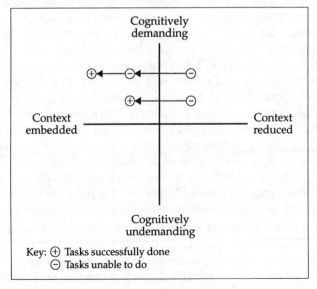

Figure 5.2 A child with language of instruction support needs

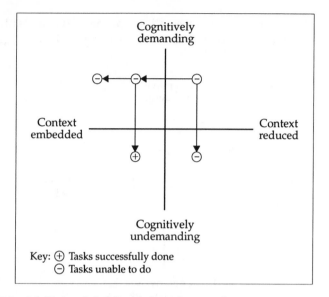

Figure 5.3 A bilingual child with learning needs

Figure 5.1 shows a profile indicative of a child with learning needs. Providing increasing degrees of contextual embedding does not assist the child in achieving success. However, reducing the cognitive demand of the task, i.e. making it easier, does allow the child to succeed. By contrast Figure 5.2 shows a profile indicative of a child with language of instruction support needs, for whom increasing degrees of contextual embedding allow success to be achieved. Typically however those bilingual children who have learning needs will also present with language needs because their general learning difficulties will also affect their learning of the language of instruction – at least their acquisition of cognitive academic aspects of language proficiency (Cummins, 1984). Hence Figure 5.3 shows a profile likely to be indicative of a bilingual child who has learning needs. For these children to achieve success they will need to be provided both with tasks at an appropriate level of difficulty in respect of their learning needs and with tasks which are appropriately contextually embedded in respect of their language needs. Once again this points to the importance of learning and language specialists working effectively together.

Figures 5.1 to 5.3 provide schematic representations of the use of the Cummins framework as an aid to decision making which beg many practical questions. These are addressed in this chapter through the first two of the four case studies provided. The last two case studies also make important points. Case Study 3 illustrates the need to consider a range of hypotheses for apparent poor progress by bilingual pupils, other than the two which form the main focus of this chapter. It is not sufficient to consider only possible learning difficulties and possible language needs. As discussed in Section 1, there is a considerable range of other possible factors that might be playing a part in creating the children's difficulties. For example, do they experience the ethos or curriculum of the school as challenging and alien rather than welcoming and accommodating? Do they have a good conversational level of English which has misled teachers into setting tasks that are too abstract for their current language level? Have they missed many experiences that others in the class have had. Are they learning now at an appropriate rate and slowly catching up? Are they subject to particular environmental stress, including experience of racism? See Wright (1991) for a detailed discussion of these hypotheses and ways in which special educational professionals can collect information to test them. Although the learning/language needs decision represents a major preoccupation of those involved in special education assessments of bilingual children, care must be taken to first consider and eliminate other possibilities. Case Study 3 underlines this point.

Case Study 4 provides a timely reminder that a child's bilingualism should not divert special education professionals from a comprehensive assessment of their needs. There is no reason to suppose that bilingual children are any less likely to be affected by sensory or learning disabilities than are monolingual children.

The chapter begins by providing some background information about the English county involved and the service structure which incorporates learning and language specialists.

The Leicestershire Approach

Background information

Leicestershire is an English county rich in cultural diversity. Twenty five percent of the population are Asian. The annual intake of pupils within many of the Leicester City schools is such that 50% speak languages other than English. The 1991 census figures for Leicester City show that Asians make up 22.1% of the city population but in some areas of the city the proportion is much higher. The main first language in Leicestershire schools other than English is Gujerati which is spoken by 14.8% of the population. Punjabi is spoken by 4% and Kutchi by 1%. Some of the inner city Leicestershire schools have as many as 97% Gujerati speakers. To have difficulties in such a setting may be different from that of the sole Gujerati speaking child in a rural area or in a small market town.

Service structure and operation

Since 1984 the Leicestershire Educational Psychology Service has been fortunate to have two bilingual support teachers to work with Educational Psychologists in assessing the needs of children (Cassell & Pratten, 1986). Initially these teachers were designated as Teacher Interpreters, supporting psychologists in their work with non–English speaking children and their families. The teacher's role was seen as fulfilling two main functions:

(1) direct work with children whether newly arrived or settled in to schooling, who have no adequate fluency in English. The work would provide an independent means of assessing linguistic development in the home language, (L1), as well as offering the option of remediation in specific areas in school.

(2) work with families in obtaining accurate information, in supporting the work of other professionals and in conveying knowledge to parents about the educational system.

It soon became apparent that the title Teacher Interpreter did not fully describe the role that the teachers took in their joint work with the educational psychologists. They were more important than interpreters of languages, having a knowledge of culture, religion and social circumstances and the expectations of the minority groups, that indirectly contributed to the effective counselling of families. The bilingual support teachers also had teaching experience across the whole age range. The referrals to the bilingual support teachers have been closely monitored over the years since 1984. Cases were categorised as follows:

(1) work related to legal assessment of special educational needs

(2) school based work accompanying an educational psychologist

(3) family work accompanying an educational psychologist

(4) family work accompanying a social worker

(5) independent family work

(6) independent teaching/counselling

Much of the casework has been dominated by activities related to legal assessment of special educational needs and by work with the educational psychologist in schools (categories 1 and 2). The psychologist and the teacher will collect information about the child's experiences and home circumstances that may or may not be factors influencing their learning. Examples of the sort of information collected are described by Desforges & Kerr (1984). The bilingual support teacher, in consultation with the educational psychologist, will undertake a trial teaching programme to assess whether the child's rate of learning is slower than that of other children of his/her age in the same class or school, or whether age appropriate rates of learning can be achieved with the provision of appropriate contextual support.

Initial assessment sessions where the child is put at ease by the teacher are undertaken. The rapport that is established between a child and an adult who identifies with the child in terms of language and culture is very important. The psychologist is able to take on the role of an observer while the teacher plays with and/or teaches the child. Often after this assessment, an individual trial teaching programme conducted at home or at school is undertaken. In consultation with the educational psychologist, targets are identified to be taught over a set period. Usually this is for some 3 to 6 one hour sessions, and the child's rate of learning is assessed over this period. The instructions for these sessions can be in the child's home language (L1), dual language (L1+L2) or the child's preferred language. Whenever possible the targets are put into the structure of the Cummins framework as illustrated by the following case studies.

Case Studies

Case Study 1

Six-year-old boy – Gujerati, no pre–school education experience.

Reason for referral – to establish whether the child has learning difficulties that require formal assessment under British special education legislation.

Targets:

(a) naming different rooms in the home

(b) three initial letter sounds to be taught

(c) drawing and naming shapes

The baseline is that the child only knows the initial letter sound 'a'.

In the Cummins framework these targets would be cognitively demanding and not context embedded. Working with the class teacher the bilingual support teacher observed that the theme in the lessons was all about the home. The bilingual support teacher provided an activity book with acetate peeling stick drawings. This was used as the medium to provide context embedded experiences for the child to name the objects and to make him aware of the initial letter sounds. In English, the bilingual support teacher found that the child did not know the word 'cooker'. In Gujerati, the bilingual support teacher found that the child identified the item from the question 'Where does your mum cook?'. Only when she had made a home visit did the bilingual support teacher discover that the family used the word 'gas' to describe their cooking appliance. Many families would associate the word 'cooker' with pressure cooker rather than stove or range. In discussion with the mother the bilingual support teacher now uses vocabulary used within the home setting. The work of teaching the initial letter sounds was reinforced at home by the mother using games such as I spy.

Having context embedded the material appropriate to the culture and environment, the bilingual support teacher was able to demonstrate that this child's rate of learning was such that he did not require formal assessment. The child was able to identify the common shapes found within his own home, name the different rooms and initial letter sounds, and therefore it was demonstrated that he did not have a significant learning difficulty. This case study therefore illustrates the schematic representation depicted in Figure 5.2.

Case Study 2

An eleven-year-old boy – from a Punjabi speaking family.

Reason for referral – learning difficulties in the first year of secondary school.

Previous experience – early schooling in India. Language of instruction Hindi. Dropped out of school because of learning and behavioural difficulties. Mother remarried a Gujerati speaking husband, and the family came to England. The child had not spoken English before he was 11 years old.

Reason for referral – the school staff were concerned about the child's learning difficulties. The bilingual support teacher initially worked both in Hindi and Punjabi to establish the following targets.

Targets:

(a) to write first name

(b) to develop word recognition skills

(c) to use common nouns in English.

The last target was addressed first. Initially the child was taught solely in Hindi. Through stories from his own experience the bilingual support teacher introduced a basic vocabulary in English. After the teaching sessions it was demonstrated that the boy was capable of learning, though at a much slower rate than his peers even with a high level of contextual embedding. Use of the Cummins grid in this case indicated that it was not possible to ensure the child's success with an age appropriate learning task simply by moving horizontally across the framework and providing more contextual support. Rather it was necessary first to move vertically down the framework in identifying easier small steps to the target. In addition it was still found necessary to ensure that these easier tasks were well embedded in context. Case Study 2 therefore illustrates the schematic representation depicted in Figure 5.3.

Case Study 3

Ten-year-old boy – Gujerati speaker

Reason for referral – reluctance to speak English. School querying learning/emotional difficulties.

Came to England when seven years old. Did not attend school in England for eighteen months. Initial assessment by the psychologist showed that non–verbal tasks could be completed at an age appropriate level. However the child refused to respond to verbal commands, requests and instructions.

Assessment by the bilingual support teacher demonstrated that the child had fluency in both written and spoken Gujerati. He was able to describe his feelings and explain that he had no need to learn English as his brother and classmates explained everything he needed to know. This child demonstrated his ability in other settings. He had swiftly established a reputation on the estate where he lived as a skilled trader in toys, bikes and computer games with older youths. Having advised his school that the child did not have learning difficulties, no intervention was attempted by the Educational Psychology Service.

A case follow up three years later found that the child is making good progress in secondary school and is no longer reluctant to use English.

This case emphasises the need to take emotional and cultural factors into account. It is not always necessary to provide intensive teaching pro-grammes. Acknowledging the child's individual needs, motivation and learning style is as important as is providing materials that are culturally appropriate and context embedded.

Case Study 4

Five-year-old girl – Gujerati speaking

Previous experience – She had pre–school experience and was identified in the nursery as having visual difficulties.

Social factors – the girl was born prematurely, and the father left the household immediately after the child was born, denying the paternity of the child. The mother was isolated from the community and had extremely limited English.

Reason for referral – Learning difficulties. Her school teachers commented that the child was not coping in a mainstream primary school. She frequently was lost within the school. The child was totally fluent in Gujerati and the bilingual support teacher swiftly established that the child had the target concepts in her first language (L1).

Targets were identified as the teaching of the days of the week and number skills.

A programme was established with her mother repeating the work that the bilingual support teacher carried out in school. This involved sequencing, days of the week and number work being taught in both languages. Neither the school nor the mother had been aware that the materials had to be modified to take account of the visual impairment that the child had.

This child was formally assessed and received teaching support but continued to make progress within the mainstream setting. Now the mother is able to cope with and help her daughter as well as acquiring English herself.

This case illustrates that when fundamental errors are made in the assessment of a child's needs, simply working through their first language in the first instance may help to identify the error, rendering use of Cummins' framework unnecessary.

Conclusions

The Bullock Report (DES, 1975) acknowledged the value of bilingualism for children as well as adults as it argued that:

> bilingualism is of great importance to the children and their families and also to society as a whole . . . No child should be expected to cast off the language and culture of the home as he crosses the threshold.

However in schools children's bilingualism is often referred to as if it were a problem or disadvantage. Gill *et al.* (1992) report that teachers often hold negative attitudes, believing that a child's other preferred language will interfere with his/her learning of English. If a bilingual child fails to grasp an apparently simple task such as counting, this may be interpreted as indicating a special educational need rather than as suggesting some difficulty in the comprehension of English.

So often special education professionals are seeking first to assess the nature of the child's difficulty and then to change how classroom teachers perceive a bilingual child. As has been shown in this chapter the Cummins framework has a contribution to make in providing an analysis of relevant tasks in assessing the child's level of learning and language proficiency. In addition, reference to the framework can also be made in helping the class teacher to identify appropriate materials and ways of teaching to meet the child's needs and offer them appropriate intellectual challenge.

But a framework of this kind is not enough on its own. As Case Studies 3 and 4 illustrate, social and cultural factors, personal history and cognitive styles of learning must also be considered. Curriculum related assessment must be applied in the context of the child's whole experience of learning and of school. Special education professionals must bring the full range of their expertise to the assessment of bilingual children, and they must consider a wide variety of possible hypotheses in seeking to understand any difficulties being experienced. The decision between a learning and a language need is an important one which can be substantially aided by consideration of the Cummins framework. However, as the case studies in this chapter have illustrated, there are other important questions to be asked and answered by special education professionals working with bilingual children.

References

Cassell, C. and Pratten, A.R. (1986) The role of teacher interpreters in a schools psychological service. *Association of Educational Psychologists Journal* Vol I.

Cline, T. and Frederickson, N. (1991) *Bilingual Pupils and the National Curriculum: Overcoming Difficulties in Teaching and Learning*. London: University College London.

Cummins, J. (1984) *Bilingualism and Special Education: Issues in Assessment and Pedagogy*. Clevedon: Multilingual Matters.

Department of Education and Science (DES) (1975) *A Language for Life* (The Bullock Report). London: HMSO.

Desforges, M. F., and Kerr, T. (1984) *Developing Bilingual Children's English in School*. Sheffield Schools Psychological Service.

Gill, D., Nayor, B. and Blair, M. (1992) *Racism and Education – Structures and Strategies*. Milton Keynes: Open University Press.

Wright, A.K. (1991) The assessment of bilingual pupils with reported learning difficulties: A hypothesis-testing approach. In T. Cline and N. Frederickson (eds) *Bilingual Pupils and the National Curriculum: Overcoming Difficulties in Teaching and Learning* (pp.185–92). London: University College London.

6 The Application of Cummins' Model to Work with Students with Hearing Impairment

ANN ROBSON

Introduction

In the past deaf people were thought of as defective monolinguals. A low value was attached to the linguistic status of sign language and to its social value. Now an increasing number of educationalists set the ultimate goal for deaf education as bilingual proficiency in a sign language and a national language. If that is not possible, a strong communicative competence in sign language will be preferable to a very limited proficiency in an oral language. So our understanding of language proficiency among deaf people increasingly depends on ideas about bilingualism. Could it be that a model that was developed to assist understanding the learning needs of children from linguistic minorities could shed some light on the way forward for this group too? Ann Robson has examined some North American work on the subject and suggests that the Cummins framework may be of great value in this context.

Factors that Affect the Learning of Children with Hearing Impairment

The basic Cummins framework is outlined in previous chapters. It has various applications for both psychologists and teachers. The main focus of this chapter is on applications to work with deaf and partially hearing students. I shall present an account of work undertaken in the United States by Barbara Luetke-Stahlman in this area.

Before considering how the Cummins framework may be applied in work with deaf pupils, it is necessary to highlight some important factors that affect the learning of the deaf. Firstly, there is research evidence that deaf children who have deaf parents have some educational advantages. For example, in acquiring language, we know from quite extensive research in deaf education that these pupils appear to have potential for a much stronger language foundation and are likely to proceed to more efficient levels of language usage and processing in advance of deaf students of hearing parents.

There is evidence that sign language is just as rule governed and logical as oral English and that sign language acquired in deaf homes follows the same developmental stages as does the speech and language of any hearing students. So it should come as no surprise that research consistently points to deaf students of deaf parents as performing significantly better in academic tasks than deaf students of hearing parents (Luetke-Stahlman, 1991).

Cummins (1984) also comments that: 'Attitude and emotional factors are likely to contribute to these differences in addition to conceptual/linguistic factors; however, the data are readily interpretable within the common underlying proficiency model of bilingualism . . . They are also precisely what one would predict on the basis of Wells' (1981) findings regarding the importance of communication in the home for later academic develop-ment.' (p. 213)

Secondly, the stage at which oral language may be lost is crucial in considering functional communication for hearing impaired pupils. For example, some children may experience normal language acquisition until an illness such as meningitis affects their hearing so that oral language subsequently deteriorates. Other students may be partially hearing but experience either slow or rapid deterioration in hearing levels which is likely to result in a similar deterioration in spoken language capability. Hence the 'Dual Iceberg' model is helpful in identifying where spoken English has been affirmed as a first language for these students. This, of course, proves beneficial where young students have subsequently to use British Sign Language as an additional language.

Thirdly, deaf children *can* develop the firm language base delineated in the 'Dual Iceberg' model, but how far they do so will depend on whether hearing aids are employed consistently and successfully to make the fullest use possible of any residual hearing ability that they have. This will considerably influence both surface features of language and underlying structures relevant to inner language and thought.

Applying Cummins' Model to Children with Hearing Impairment

Turning to applications of Cummins' model to deaf and partially hearing students, it is the American commentary and research which offers the most helpful work to date and is reported here. In particular, Barbara Luetke-Stahlman and John Luckner of the Northern Illinois University have been pioneers in applying Cummins' model to work with hearing impaired and deaf students. Recognising the implications of cognition and context, Luetke-Stahlman suggests that because Cummins' model is based on research with hearing children from bilingual backgrounds, it may be a useful model for discussing assessment or for task analysis in relation to hearing impaired students. She also suggests that methods traditionally used to assess bilingual hearing impaired students include features that are also found in Cummins' model of bilingual proficiency (1984).

Further, she suggests that task analysis based on the Cummins' model also ensures that teachers will be prepared to individualise teaching programmes and tasks according to the particular needs of students. For example, when working on language forms with children she suggests a good rule of thumb to keep in mind is for the teacher to move up the vertical axis, beginning with the concrete, literal applications of target structures. Then the teacher may move to more abstract or figurative levels as students develop their awareness of the structure. She suggests that language work should always progress from the concrete and literal to the abstract and from immediate experience to vicarious experience (i.e. from what is context-embedded and cognitively undemanding to what is context-reduced and cognitively demanding).

Luetke-Stahlman & Luckner (1991) also offer a variation of Cummins' model in considering speech development and language proficiency (see Figure 6.1). This is utilised to encourage children to employ correct speech patterns that have been taught at the phonetic level in gradually broader, more demanding contexts of meaningful speech. Hence speech development and language in context are mapped on to the model to demonstrate how skills taught at the phonetic level can be applied in real contexts as automatic transfer from one to the other is so hard to achieve.

For the purposes of this chapter, two areas of Luetke-Stahlman's applications are considered in detail, these being auditory training and speech reading assessment. First, the role of auditory training is considered. The majority of hearing impaired pupils have sufficient residual hearing so that they can usefully benefit from wearing hearing aids. However, we know that wearing a hearing aid is not a sufficient condition to guarantee

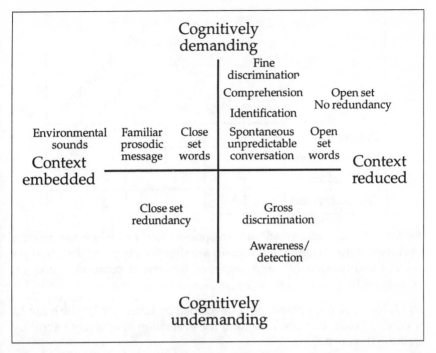

Figure 6.1 Cummins' model of language proficiency adapted for speech articulation (Luetke-Stahlman & Luckner, 1991)

that students will optimise their auditory capacity. In addition to appropriate hearing aids, students need good audiological management, support and education from relevant adults and auditory experiences of spoken language which are meaningful and appropriate to their age and interests (Bunch, 1987). Here, auditory training involves teaching students to listen and make use of their residual hearing at at least four different levels – detecting sounds, discriminating between sounds, identifying auditory patterns and comprehending their meaning (Ling, 1986). Hence listening differs from hearing in the degree of understanding and effort involved. Auditory training supplements the auditory experience of hearing impaired pupils, allowing skills which are not learned in a natural way to be developed systematically in a more structured environment.

Bearing this in mind, one application of Cummins' model presented by Luetke-Stahlman is relevant to auditory training and to the important question of how teachers may assess students' auditory abilities in order to plan their training. She suggests that teachers plot each student's aided and unaided acuity on an audiogram, using both formal and informal assess-

	Speech elements	Syllabus	Words	Phrases	Sentences	Connected discourse
Detection	1					
Discrimination						
Identification			2			
Comprehension					3	

Figure 6.2 An auditory stimulus-response matrix in which the relative positions of three cognitive processes are shown – phoneme detection (1), word identification (2), and sentence (question) comprehension (3) (Erber, 1982)

ment. Next she presents a matrix developed by Erber (1982) which can be used as a guide to intervention and the evaluation of aspects of auditory training (Figure 6.2).

In this matrix teachers can indicate whether a student can respond to speech stimuli as they become longer and linguistically more complex. They can also indicate whether the student can respond to speech stimuli solely as sounds or in terms of their language value and meaning as well.

Erber's concept levels has been subsequently grafted onto Cummins' Model of language proficiency.

Use of this model helped teachers to predict which students can discriminate familiar sounds in a closed set only (bottom left quadrant of Figure 6.1), and hence will not be able to function without a visual mode of support in an academic situation. A student who can comprehend open set teacher instructions (top right quadrant) should be able to be placed in a hearing classroom on a trial basis and monitored to see whether simultaneous communication support is needed (Luetke-Stahlman & Luckner, 1991).

Secondly, Luetke-Stahlman developed Cummins model for application in speech reading assessment. Speech reading refers to the process of understanding a spoken message through the observation of the speaker's face, commonly known as lip reading. Luetke-Stahlman (1991) suggests that ' . . . when existing speech reading tests are organised by quadrant

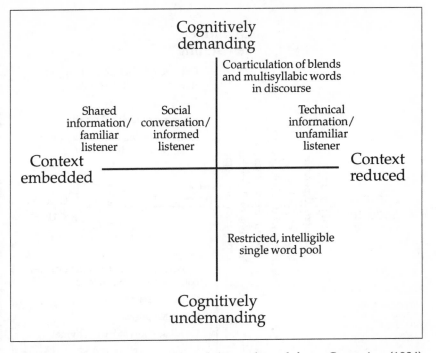

Figure 6.3 Auditory perception ability, adapted from Cummins (1984) (Luetke-Stahlman & Luckner, 1991)

constraints from the Cummins' Model, it appears that a complete speech reading evaluation of hearing impaired students cannot be conducted without additional test development'. This is relevant, for example, when we consider apparently contradictory findings when students can speech read successfully in one context (e.g. with a therapist) but not in another (e.g. in classroom presentations). Hence, Luetke-Stahlman suggests teachers would benefit from using speech reading evaluation tools in several contexts. This would also provide information about a student's strengths as well as weaknesses.

The Erber Model (outlined previously) may assist teachers in adapting communication tasks for the student who is having speech reading difficulties by systematically altering the task demands. But Luetke-Stahlman demonstrates through another adaptation of the Cummins framework that it is again possible to use the Cummins model of language proficiency to clarify the task demands further. An assessment of speech reading abilities can be seen in terms of the contextual support that is available and of the cognitive demands that are made during the task.

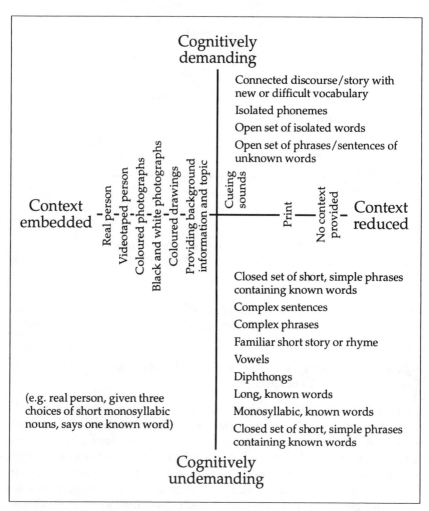

Figure 6.4 The Cummins (1984) model of language proficiency with speech reading tasks incorporated (Luetke-Stahlman & Luckner, 1991)

Within the Cummins model, the cognitive linguistic demand of the speech reading task is defined as the syntax and semantic difficulties of the stimulus language. Luetke-Stahlman suggests that an advantage of using the adapted Cummins model over the Erber model is that the former allows for a richer assessment of information which can contribute to decisions on the placement of bilingual, or bimodal students.

Finally, the benefit of using the adapted Cummins model in assessing speech reading ability in twelve hearing impaired students was tested in a

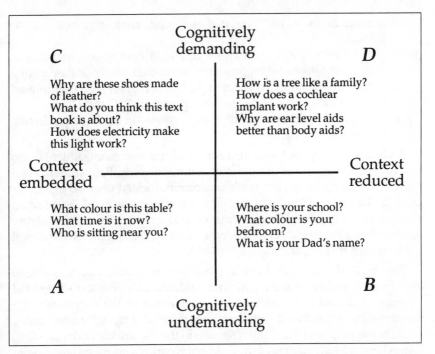

Figure 6.5 Questions used in speech reading assessment of hearing impaired students (adapted from Luetke-Stahlman & Luckner, 1991)

tutorial situation by Luetke-Stahlman and college trainees who were studying to become teachers of the deaf. Three questions were generated to reflect the age and interest of particular hearing impaired students who also attended regular clinic sessions. Questions included each of the combinations of high and low context and high and low cognitive/linguistic demand in the Cummins model. Cognitively demanding questions were longer than those which were cognitively undemanding and involved higher cognitive processing skills. This meant that a set of individual questions was used with each hearing impaired student, but all questions conformed to the Cummins quadrant constraints (see examples of the questions in Figure 6.5).

Each student was asked to speech read a random ordering of the questions, which were asked once each without voice, during weekly sessions. Data was recorded for each question asked at least three times over three consecutive sessions. The index of successful speech reading was a clear attempt to answer the question. Results of this small study were:

(a) Eleven out of the twelve hearing impaired students could answer the questions in the cognitively undemanding, context embedded (A) quadrant.

(b) Eight of the twelve students were able to answer questions asked in oral English (alone) when questions were cognitively undemanding and context embedded (quadrant A) but not when they exemplified other points along the two continua (quadrants B, C and D).

(c) One student could answer all the questions (in all four quadrants) asked in oral English.

A variation of this task was also run involving two more students who had different preferences in modes of communication. Both students had profound hearing losses, but while one communicated unaided in American Sign Language (ASL), the second wore aids, made good use of some residual hearing and was mainstreamed into a university course, relying on speech to communicate. In this case multi-modal questions were used (ASL, speech reading and signed English).

The results demonstrated that the student who used speech was able to answer all questions in the cognitively undemanding, context embedded situation and could comprehend speech reading in the cognitively demanding, context reduced situation (bottom left and top right quadrants), while her signing peer had similar success in the cognitively undemanding, context embedded quadrant but could not comprehend speech reading in the cognitively demanding, context reduced situation.

Luetke-Stahlman suggests that Cummins' work (1984) with hearing bilingual students also evidenced this type of behaviour in that he found some Spanish speaking students perplexed teachers because they could understand English in some conversational situations (quadrant A) but not in academic ones (quadrant D) (Luetke-Stahlman, 1991).

In summary, then, Cummins' (1984) Model suggests that first language quadrant D behaviours should be assessed to predict second language quadrant D abilities. Luetke-Stahlman suggests that this can be extended to the communication systems employed by hearing impaired pupils. It seems necessary to suppose that since English is probably not the first language of all hearing impaired students, an age-appropriate complete quadrant D language base needs to be developed on which to build English literacy skills. Hearing impaired students are given the opportunity to demonstrate which language or communication system is the most beneficial for them in acquiring cognitive academic skills, then classroom placement should be based on these findings. For example, sign dominant students should be provided with sign dominant instruction, system dominant students should be provided with accurate, consistently signed

English language models, and cueing or oral dominant students should be provided with an accurate, proficient cued or oral model for instruction (Luetke-Stahlman, 1991: 36-37).

The Cummins model is also demonstrated as a useful tool in organising speech reading assessment material for hearing impaired students. Teachers might benefit from categorising speech reading assessment and later intervention, with regard to context embeddedness and cognitive-linguistic task demands. The value of the Cummins model in assessing language proficiency of hearing impaired students is that a multi-modal assessment can be planned rather than a monolingual or bilingual one. Further, academic goals can be organised systematically by using the four quadrants of the model.

Applications in research and classroom teaching using British Sign Language are needed to extend this work within the British context. With the introduction of the National Curriculum and Individual Education Plans for students, it appears that Cummins' basic model has much to offer in programme planning as well as assessment in work with hearing impaired students in our new era of special education provision.

References

Arnold, P. (1992) Effectively educating students with hearing impairments. *Deafness and Development* 2 (2), 24–26. University of Manchester.

Bunch, G.O. (1987) *The Curriculum and the Hearing Impaired Student: Theoretical and Practical Considerations*. Boston: Little, Brown.

Cummins, J. (1984) *Bilingualism and Special Education: Issues in Assessment and Pedagogy*. Clevedon: Multilingual Matters.

Erber, N.P. (1982) *Auditory Training*. Washington, DC: The Alexander Graham Bell Association for the Deaf.

Ling, D. (1986) Devices and procedures for auditory learning. *Voltar Review* 88 (5), 19–27.

Luetke-Stahlman, B. and Luckner, J. (eds) (1991) *Effectively Educating Students with Hearing Impairments*. New York: Longman Publishing Group.

Section 4:
Bilingual Language Development

Introduction

To understand the educational achievements of children from linguistic minority communities it is essential to develop a convincing analysis of their bilingual language development. Language is central to the education process in school. Probably it is central to all of the types of thinking and knowledge that organised schooling sets out to encourage. When children start out in school with a language that is different from the language used by their teachers, there must be a question mark over the teachers' ability to help them. Yet many children prosper academically in these circumstances, and many learn much of the classroom language that they need quite quickly. At the same time there is a good deal of evidence too that for many of the children there appears to be a ceiling on what they can achieve when the language of the classroom becomes more complex and demanding. Cummins developed his model to assist in understanding these phenomena. What evidence is there that it is useful for the specific purpose of analysing bilingual language development?

In Chapter 7 Olga Barradas describes her study of a small sample of young Portuguese children in London. She shows how Cummins' framework can help us to understand the complex patterns of their use of language. They are in a unique situation poised between two language communities – the 'Portinglês' speakers at home and the English speakers in school and elsewhere. Will they acquire competence in each of these languages in the same way? Making use of Cummins' framework Barradas shows that in her sample the superficial appearance of a balance between Portinglês and English may be misleading. She suggests that differences in the children's proficiency between languages were context-related. Hence they were prone to make different types of error in each language according to the task they were performing and the context associated with that task (e.g. home or school). Although her findings have to be treated with some caution because of the small size of the sample in the study, her conclusions are in line with those of other researchers. There are significant implications for methods of language teaching in the classroom in primary school and later (Ellis, 1987). These results also underline the value of teacher-parent partnership arrangements.

Finally in Chapter 8 Mike Haworth and John Joyce describe the use of a new resource they have developed for assessing the language skills of bilingual pupils in the classroom. In their practice as educational psychologists in schools they encountered an unexpected difficulty in using the Cummins framework for assessment and planning. They found that many of the teachers and support staff working with the children were uncertain about the limits of their language proficiency and about information on their backgrounds. These staff also found it hard sometimes to analyse the language demands of work set in the classroom. So Haworth and Joyce set out to develop a system for recording the use of language that would make it easier for staff to structure their observations of the children's proficiency and to define the language demands of the tasks the children were given. This new resource is called The Bilingual Language Assessment Record.

This Language Record builds on earlier assessment work and research in the U.K. and the U.S.A., including Mattes and Omark (1984), Tough (1976), Wells (1985) and Crystal *et al.* (1976). It consists of a summary of information on the child that may have assessment implications, a checklist of language functions (in which a record is made of children's competence in both their first and their second languages), a similar checklist of sentences and grammatical structures, and a vocabulary record in which the focus is on the use of verbs. Haworth and Joyce report that some teachers in Leeds have found the 'Functions' checklist in their Language Record easier to use in class or group planning than the Cummins framework. They suggest that this is because the Record sets out specific questions for teachers to answer whereas that framework is unspecific in terms of content.

Thus the openness and flexibility of the framework which were welcomed by some other chapter authors are seen to have some disadvantages in this context. For Haworth and Joyce the model appears to come into its own at a different stage – when developing practical language activities for the classroom that will be both intellectually demanding and context-embedded. In a book that is largely dedicated to exploring the value of a particular individual model for assessment it is fitting that the final chapter should illustrate that (a) the world of assessment does not begin and end with that model and (b) there is a contribution the model can make even when other useful methods of assessment are employed.

References

Crystal, D., Fletcher, P. and Garman, M. (1976) *The Grammatical Analysis of Language Disability: A Procedure for Assessment and Remediation*. London: Edward Arnold.

Ellis, R. (1987) Contextual variability in second language acquisition and the relevancy of language teaching. In R. Ellis (ed.) *Second Language Acquisition in Context*. Hemel Hempstead, Hertfordshire: Prentice-Hall International (UK).

Mattes, L.J. and Omark, D.R. (1984) *Speech and Language Assessment for the Bilingual Handicapped*. San Diego: College Hill Press.

Tough, J. (1976) *Listening to Children Talking*. London: Schools Council Publications.

Wells, C.G. (1985) *Language Development in the Pre-School Years*. Cambridge: Cambridge University Press.

7 A Study of the Oral Language Proficiency of Portuguese Bilingual Children in London

OLGA BARRADAS

Introduction

The study described in this chapter was carried out with bilingual Portuguese children born in the U.K. whose parents are first generation migrants.

The study's main objective was to try and assess the children's proficiency in Portuguese and in English. In order to do this it was necessary to consider not only the difficulties related to assessing language development in bilingual children, but also the children's first language which being a community language, may present characteristics that differ from those of the 'language-norm' as it is spoken in the country of origin. It is, thus, important to identify the main deviations in the child's mother tongue before making comparisons with the child's proficiency in another language.

Therefore the first part of this chapter will focus on the community from which the participants were selected and the characteristics of the variety of Portuguese spoken by this community, i.e. Portinglês. The second part of the chapter will concern the study itself and its methodology, how the language samples were collected and analysed and, finally, the results and discussion.

The Portuguese Community

The exact number of Portuguese migrants in the U.K. is difficult to assess. Estimates from sources such as the 1981 Census, the Secretary of State for Emigration and community organisations suggest that the total number of Portuguese people living in the U.K. is approximately 40,000 (Santarita & Martin-Jones, 1991). The Linguistic Minorities Project, carried out ten years ago, quoted the number of Portuguese people living in Britain as being over 30,000 (LMP, 1985).

Notwithstanding these figures, official statistics do not give us a very exact idea of the size of the community as they do not take into account British-born children nor elderly relatives who have come to join their families in the U.K. Furthermore, the number of seasonal workers in the Channel Islands is not always included.

Despite a number of Portuguese families having returned to Portugal in recent years, with Portugal's status as a full member of the European Union, the number of Portuguese people settling in Britain has continued to rise. Approximately two-thirds of the Portuguese community live in the London area, where they concentrate mostly in the areas of Kensington and Chelsea, Lambeth, Hammersmith and Fulham, Camden and Westminster.

Large numbers of Portuguese work as cleaners, domestic staff, kitchen porters and assistant cooks in the hotel and catering industries (Santarita & Martin-Jones, 1991). In these occupations, the working hours are long and antisocial and include weekends. These jobs are low-paid, and often the workers are forced to find additional employment on a shift basis to supplement their income. This leaves little time to meet people outside their own community or to learn English outside the workplace. Their knowledge of this language is, in most cases, limited to the minimal English skills necessary to carry out their daily duties.

In addition, most of the first generation migrants did not have access to post-primary education in Portugal before migrating, and few have had the chance to attend formal English classes. Thus, they tend to have considerably less confidence in their language abilities than Portuguese people who have had many more years of formal education. For this reason, in a number of situations, such as visits to the doctor, interviews related to applications for work or visits to their children's school, they find it difficult to manage. Sometimes their own children help by translating when talking to teachers, or they have to rely on interpreters and translators who are, for the most part, friends or family members rather than trained community language interpreters and translators.

Portuguese, a Romance language, developed out of the Vulgar Latin of the Roman Empire although the influence of erudite Latin can also be detected in early Portuguese writings. Portuguese was also influenced by the Arabic of the Muslim settlers who inhabited Portugal for eight centuries before being expelled in 1249. The effect on the language was mainly on the lexis, as a large number of words were borrowed for the new products and technological advances introduced.

In the fifteenth and sixteenth centuries, Portugal became a world sea power, establishing trading stations and colonies throughout the world. Today, Portuguese is the official language of Portugal, Brazil, Mozambique, Angola, Guinea-Bissau and Cape-Verde. It is estimated that, by the end of this century, Portuguese will be spoken by over 210 million people and will thus become the language with the fifth-largest number of speakers in the world (Cristovão, 1987).

In migrant communities round the world, Portuguese is spoken by approximately 4 million migrants, of which 1 million alone are in France. Other sizeable Portuguese settlements are to be found in Luxembourg (where about two per cent of the population are of Portuguese origin), in Venezuela and in parts of North America (430,000 speakers).

Over the years, a distinctive way of speaking has emerged within Portuguese speaking communities abroad. It results from the 'linguistic mixing' of two different languages, Portuguese and that of the host country. In communities living in English-speaking countries, this type of language, known as Portinglês, involves frequent borrowing and adapting of words and expressions from English into the discourse, instead of using Portuguese words and expressions with equivalent meaning. Although incomprehensible to someone foreign to the community, it is extremely well-used by its members. even by those who have a very poor knowledge of English (Mayone Dias, 1986).

In a study of language contact between Portuguese and English, Keating (1990) describes the forms of integration found in Portinglês as lexical borrowings and loan-words. Integration is defined here as the phenomenon where elements in the lexicon of one language enter into the lexicon of another, thus producing a change in the latter.

According to Poplack (1980), borrowing can be defined as involving the incorporation of Language 2 (L2) words into the discourse of Language 1 (L1), usually morphologically or phonologically adapted to conform to the pattern of that language's discourse. Loan-words would be those integrated words which would be widely used within the speech community and with a certain level of recognition or acceptance, thus not directly linked to discourse.

Loan-words can be further divided into Loan shifts (Lehiste, 1988) and Loan translations (Weinreich, 1953). In the category of loan shifts, where there is a change in the meaning of a morpheme of one language on the model of the other language (semantic shift), there can be two degrees of integration. In the first one, we can have an extension of the meaning of a word in L1, to include the meaning of another word in L2 with a similar phonetic form. An example of this extension of meaning would be the word **ordens**/orders:

Faço as **ordens** dos produtos comestíveis.
(I do the orders for food products.)
(in Keating, 1990)

This word, **ordens**, which in Portuguese means 'commands' does not have, unlike in English, a further meaning of request to supply goods. It is thus given a new meaning not existent in Standard European Portuguese, following the rules established in the English language.

A variation on this meaning extension occurs when a word in L1 acquires a polysemic status, even if the similar word in L2 does not have such a status. This happens for example, with **uva**. The meaning of the standard Portuguese 'uva' (grape) is extended to accommodate the English 'Hoover' (aspirador). A sentence incorporating **uva** with its newly acquired meaning (Hoover – aspirador) would be nonsensical to a monolingual Portuguese speaker.

A second degree of integration consists in the total semantic shift in similar forms of the two languages. Gradually, the original meaning of the word in the recipient language (L1) is completely substituted by the meaning of that word in the L2. An example of this type of total semantic shift would be the word **ofícios**:

Eu ajudo a minha mãe a limpar os **ofícios**.
(I help my Mum to clean the offices.)

The meaning of 'ofícios' (occupations or jobs) in Standard Portuguese, is taken over by that of 'offices' (escritórios).

Loan translations (Weinreich, 1953), on the other hand, consist of translating morphemes in L2 into morphemes in L1, thus creating new forms for new meanings. Sometimes, whole sentences or expressions are literally translated into L1, introducing new expressions, different from the norm. The newly obtained expressions follow the gender and number requirements of Portuguese and can be given Portuguese affixes and prefixes. The verbs, however, always belong to the Portuguese first conjugation (-**ar** ending), e.g. **parkar** (to park = estacionar) (Mayone Dias, 1986). There are some cases where loan translation is deliberately chosen to avoid similarities with certain improper words in either language. That is the case of the loan-word **naifa** (knife = faca).

Idiomatic expressions are also directly translated and linguistically adapted to the recipient language. This is the case of **deram-me o saco** (I was given the sack – Fui despedido), which in Standard Portuguese would mean 'I was given the bag'. Once more, the meaning of these loan translations in a conversation would be incomprehensible to a monolingual Standard Portuguese speaker. Their semantic value as loan translations makes them different from the norm, and they therefore constitute new idiomatic expressions with a unique meaning.

The Study

This study aimed to analyse the oral language of Portuguese English bilingual children. The study looked for a relation between the levels of proficiency shown in Portuguese and in English.

In this study, when interviewed, the parents put forward Portuguese as the main language used to communicate with the children. The children, however, use both Portuguese and English to talk to their parents and preferred English when talking to their siblings.

The sample was chosen from children attending Portuguese classes in three schools in those areas of London with large numbers of Portuguese people (the areas chosen were Fulham, Camden and Ladbroke Grove). These classes, organised by the Portuguese Consulate, take place after regular school hours, in the evening or on Saturdays. Because seven is the age at which children can start attending these classes, that was the age group chosen.

A sample of 11 children fulfilling three conditions was selected:

(a) were born in the UK in the years 1984 or 1985;

(b) were attending Portuguese classes for the first time during that school year;

(c) Portuguese parents only.

Following Cummins' (1984) framework (see Chapter 1), the study tried to compare the levels of proficiency in both English and Portuguese in the two dimensions of language use proposed by that author in terms of cognitive demand and contextual dependency. However, in view of the objectives of the study, it seemed appropriate to test the children only in cognitively demanding activities which varied along the continuum of context-embeddedness, as this is the type of activity the children are more likely to encounter in the classroom. Thus, the language samples obtained in each language referred to:

(a) an activity which is cognitively demanding but embedded in context;

(b) an activity which is cognitively demanding but context-reduced.

The activities chosen to elicit the language samples in these dimensions were (i) telling a story from a picture storybook and (ii) a jigsaw guessing game. For each language a book and a jigsaw were chosen. The picture books, without text, referred to activities familiar to all children: getting up in the morning and going to bed at night (*Sunshine, Moonlight*; Ormerod, 1982). All the writing in the books was covered to avoid suggesting a particular language to the children.

The two jigsaws depicting different pictures, of scenes unfamiliar to the children (Portuguese jigsaw 52cm x 40cm; English jigsaw 70cm x 38cm), were divided into 17 and 13 pieces. The pieces were cut in such a way as not to give away too much information at a time.

The procedure for the story-telling and jigsaw-game was the same for both Portuguese and English.[1] The activities were tape-recorded and later transcribed. The children were allowed time to familiarise themselves with the story, and then asked to give the main character a name and tell the story.

The children were also asked to participate in the jigsaw game (Jones *et al.*, 1990). The objective of this 'game' was to predict from parts of the picture what could probably be in the whole picture, thus making this a cognitively demanding task in a reduced context.

The jigsaw pieces were turned face down and numbered, so that all the children followed the same order and got the same cues from the picture. To enhance the motivation to participate and to give the activity a game-like format, 15 coloured counters were introduced. The children were given some counters which they could use to 'buy' jigsaw pieces. The remaining counters could be won by giving more information about their predictions of the whole picture. They were an extra incentive.

After transcription, the language samples were divided into utterances,[2] and these were examined for deviation under a total of nine criteria, within the three main categories of code-mixing, pragmatic criteria and syntax difficulties:

Code-mixing

Within the code-mixing category, deviations were divided into the categories of code-switch and loan-shift.

A code-switch deviation was noted when the child used complete words from language A when speaking in language B.

A loan-shift deviation was noted when the utterance contained either a loan-word or a loan-translation or both.

Pragmatic criteria

For this criterion, the definitions used by Damico *et al.* (1983) were followed. However, instead of the seven categories those authors had used, only three seemed appropriate to the kind of difficulties the subjects were more likely to exhibit. These were linguistic non-fluencies, revisions and non-specific vocabulary.

(a) *Linguistic non-fluencies*

Production is disrupted by repetitions, unusual pauses (over 7 sec.), and hesitation phenomena. (e.g. And she looks . . . and she . . .).

(b) *Revisions*

The child seems to come to dead ends in a maze, as if starting off in a certain direction, then coming back to the starting point and beginning anew after each attempt. (e.g. His Dad – Her Dad – Zara's Dad was reading a book.)

(c) *Non-specific vocabulary*

Use of terms such as *this, then, there,* pronominals, proper nouns, and possessives when no such antecedent can readily be inferred by the listener. Children displaying this difficulty also tend to overuse generic terms such as *thing* and *stuff.* (e.g. and . . . and she's in the little *thing* at the back of *it,* the . . . like a trolley.)

Syntax difficulties

Within this type of difficulty, four criteria were chosen: Gender error, number error, possessives and verb error.

(a) Gender errors included all deviations in gender whether they referred to nouns, adjectives, pronouns or verbs.

(b) Number errors included all deviations in number whether they referred to nouns, adjectives or pronouns.

(c) Errors in the use of forms of the possessive.

(d) Verb errors included all deviations in tense in regular and irregular verbs, agreement number-verb (1st, 2nd, 3rd person/singular, plural).

Results

The study looked for differences between the two languages (English and Portuguese) and between the tasks and error categories.

With regard to the total number of utterances produced by the children, the samples in the two languages did not show a significant difference. Taking the two languages together and comparing the total number of utterances in the two tasks, it was found that the jigsaw task elicited a significantly higher number of utterances than the story telling task. This is probably caused by the characteristics of the task itself. The components of the jigsaw elicit more talk, and this is enhanced by 'rewarding' the children with counters (see Figure 7.1).

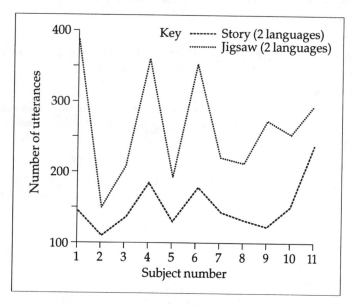

Figure 7.1 Total Number of Utterances Between Tasks

Large variations were found in the number of errors obtained. These wide variations occurred between tasks and between and within error categories. For example, the same child had as many as 49 errors in one category (linguistic non-fluency) but only four in another one (non-specific vocabulary), both within the same error category (pragmatic type of error).

For this reason the nine categories were collapsed into the three main categories of error: code-mixing, pragmatic criteria and syntax difficulties.

The values obtained were then used to make comparisons:

(a) between the two languages (total value of errors for each language), and

(b) between the two tasks.

For the tasks, a 'cross-analysis' was used.

The two tasks were compared against each other, within each language and then against tasks in the other language. Thus, for example, the results obtained in the Portuguese jigsaw were compared with the results obtained in the Portuguese story and then each task was compared with the results obtained in the English versions. Finally,

(c) an even more detailed analysis was obtained by comparing the categories of error between themselves for each language, both within each task and between tasks, and then cross-comparing against the categories of error for the tasks in the other language.[3]

The elements in these comparisons could be visualised as shown below:

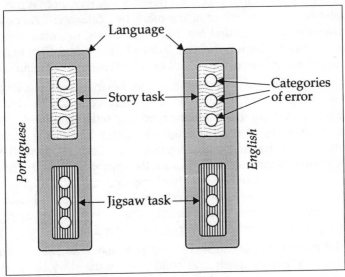

Figure 7.2 Representations of the factors analysed

The results obtained, adding all categories of error and comparing the total number of errors in one language against the total number in the other (analysis A: language vs language), showed that no statistically significant differences were found between the total number of errors produced in the two languages.

However, when we separated the error scores for each of the tasks (analysis B: task vs task), we found quite different results. The statistical analysis revealed a pattern of error associating a language and a type of task (Interaction Language x Task: $F = 4.97$; d.f. 1, 10, $p<0.05$).

In the jigsaw task, the error scores obtained in the English task were significantly lower than in the corresponding Portuguese version of the task. Thus, when doing the task that had been considered more difficult, the children performed better in their second language than in their mother tongue.

On the other hand, in the English story task a significantly larger number of errors were obtained than in the Portuguese story task. Thus, in the 'easier' task, the children showed more difficulty in English than in Portuguese.

When the error categories were compared within each of the tasks (analysis C: categories of error vs. categories of error), it was found that, in all situations, the children produced overwhelmingly more errors of the pragmatic type than of either of the other two categories. As described above, this category included revisions, hesitations, repetitions and non-specific vocabulary. Damico *et al.* (1983) describe these deviations as possible indicators of a language disorder, apt to have academic consequences.

However, in the case of the bilingual children in this sample, it was felt that this interpretation might not be entirely correct. The deviations categorised as being of the pragmatic type may reflect children's thinking and their processes of self-correction. In order to avoid a code or a syntax-type error, the child might stop in the middle of a sentence. Because s/he may not remember, or not yet know, the appropriate word s/he needs to express the ideas correctly in either language, the child might have to interrupt her/himself abruptly and reformulate a sentence. This would not reflect a linguistic problem but merely the process of acquiring new vocabulary for both languages (Portuguese or/and English).

On the other hand, the design of the task may lend itself to error of reference. Both experimenter and child can see the story book and the jigsaw that is being completed in front of them, so it would be logical for the child to assume that, in using pronouns, its referent would be understood by the interviewer. To eliminate this possibility, the materials would have to be in such a position that they could be seen by the child but not by the interviewer. The child would then have to make explicit reference to nouns to make the ideas understood by the interviewer. Only if it could be ascertained that it would not be reasonable for the child to assume full comprehension by the interviewer of the subject of their conversation could the use of pronouns be considered a pragmatic error.[4]

For these reasons, the pragmatic category was excluded from further analysis of the error scores.

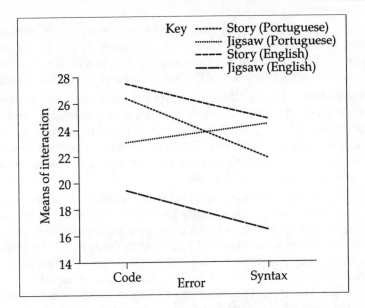

Figure 7.3 Means of interactions: factors language x task x error

The analysis of the language samples also revealed an interesting association between the categories of errors elicited and the other two factors: task and language. It was found that, in both languages, the story task elicited more code than syntax errors.

However, we have a different result for the jigsaw task. While in the English syntax the children show relative facility, on the other hand, in Portuguese, their mother tongue, they show a greater difficulty. If we take a look at the above illustration (Figure 7.3), it is clear that the children's syntax errors are lower than their code errors in all tasks, except the Portuguese jigsaw.

Discussion

By comparing the total error scores we have found that the children had approximately similar scores in both languages, thus suggesting that an equivalent level of linguistic competence had been attained in the two languages.

Cummins (1981) has suggested that five to seven years are needed after introduction to the second language to reach adequate levels of competency to allow complex functions in a second language. In the case of these children, similar error scores in both English and Portuguese could be the result of having been born in this country and, therefore, having not only been exposed to the English language in the environment but also of having, at least, two years of English schooling. Seven of the eleven children had attended nursery from about three years of age, thus having experienced about four years of English schooling by the time of testing.

These children were, therefore, probably well into the process of understanding and acquiring more complex semantic features and functional meaning in English than if they had come from Portugal at the equivalent starting school age. One may, therefore, suggest that these children do not need such a long period of time to develop their proficiency in more complex aspects of English.

This argument could also be used to justify the difference found between the jigsaw tasks, where significantly lower error scores were obtained in the English jigsaw task than in the corresponding Portuguese version of the task. Children's experience of schooling in English and the language skills thus developed probably facilitate the children's performance in an activity which requires predicting, hypothesising and adjusting to new information. This type of activity is more likely to be encountered at school. Thus, the type of language involved is more likely to be acquired or developed first in the school language (English) and then in the home language (Portuguese).

The results found also showed that the English story task is associated with a significantly greater number of errors than the Portuguese story task. The reason for this difference may be related to familiarity with the subject matter of the books. This familiarity is not so much with the type of task nor with the materials, but with the context described in each of the two stories. The stories referred to the rituals of getting up in the morning, going to bed in the evening; activities which constitute an integral part of the children's day-to-day experience, at home, with their Portuguese-speaking parents.

Therefore, it may be that the context-embeddedness of the story task facilitates the children's performance in Portuguese at a double level. Firstly, because the context of the story is familiar and secondly, because, for these children, it occurs only (or almost exclusively) in Portuguese.

This strong association with the home language, Portuguese, raises an important issue. If we consider, as suggested by Keating (1990) and by Mayone-Dias (1986), that the language used at home may include a lot of Portinglês, then it would only be natural for the children's language to reflect this type of 'interference'.

If we accept this argument, how can we consider code-mixing a linguistic error in a language sample, if we take that sample from a community where code-mixing is accepted and commonly used by its members?

On the other hand, the type of language used in the community is not so organised nor so rich and complex that it may allow the creation of a grammatical/lexical system independent from the Portuguese language. (Portuguese here refers to the language as spoken in Portugal). Therefore, when we compare the results obtained in this language sample with the norm-Portuguese, we might consider the proportion of code-mixing errors unacceptable. If, nevertheless, we consider that Portinglês is probably widely used at home the proportion of 'error' will be justifiable.

It is, thus, possible that there may be a link between the language spoken at home and the children's code-error scores in both stories. But why did the children, in English, produce more code errors than syntax errors in both tasks, story and jigsaw?

As discussed above, the children's performance in the story task could be affected by the story-context and the type of language spoken at home. It could also be that their English schooling was having a strong positive effect in their syntax development, as the type of language elicited by the jigsaw task is more likely to be found and developed in school activities. Thus, if we take the possibility that schooling could have a positive effect in the syntax of the language elicited through the school type of activity (jigsaw) it follows that, in the language where the children had less school experience, their syntax would show more errors. This corresponds to the results obtained in the Portuguese jigsaw.

Conclusion

The main conclusion obtained from this study is that, although these children appear to have reached an equilibrated level of bilingualism in Portuguese and in English, when we compare different situations and types of task, a different picture emerges. Different contexts may be associated with different languages and, for each language, different tasks elicit different types of error. A child who performs very well according to certain parameters in a given task, may not perform as well in another task.

Finally, as expected, the positive effect of early schooling can be seen in the children's performance in English, the language in which they have school experience. This seems to indicate a need for earlier schooling in the child's mother tongue. If the children had had access to nursery schools where they could have developed their Portuguese language skills and experience the type of activities associated with the English classroom, their performance in the less context-embedded tasks might have been even better.

114 CURRICULUM RELATED ASSESSMENT

Acknowledgements

I would like to thank Angela Hobsbaum for helpful discussions and encouragement and Dr. John Versey for expert input with the statistical analysis.

Notes

1. The tasks for Portuguese and English were conducted by native speakers of each language.
2. An utterance was taken to be any meaningful communication unit carrying a distinct and unified propositional meaning, even though it may not appear between clear phonological junctures. In doubtful cases opening and closing contours were followed.
3. In order to allow an analysis of all three main error categories, the scores were converted to proportions of the total number of deviations in each sample, thus obtaining an 'error score' for each category. The 'error scores' obtained were then transformed from proportional measures (errors/total responses) employing Arcsin equivalents to counteract any problems with variances (Winer, 1971) and used in a three-way analysis of variance. The factors analysed in this test were the two languages, the two types of task and, within each task, the three categories of error.
4. For the reasons explained, since the values being analysed are proportions and the pragmatic category of error was significantly larger than the other categories, it had to be removed from the analysis. Therefore, another three-way analysis of variance was done with only two main categories of error: code errors and syntax errors. The results obtained in this analysis confirmed those obtained in the first one.

References

Barradas, O. (1993) A study of the oral language of Portuguese bilingual children in London. Unpublished MA Dissertation, Institute of Education, University of London.

Cristovão, F. (1987) *Notícias e Problemas da Pátria da Lingua*. Lisboa: Instituto de Cultura e Língua Portuguesa.

Cummins, J. (1981) Age on arrival and immigrant second language learning in Canada: A reassessment. *Applied Linguistics* 2, 132–149.

— (1984) *Bilingualism and Special Education: Issues in Assessment and Pedagogy*. Clevedon: Multilingual Matters.

Damico, J. S., Oller, J. W. and Storey, M. E. (1983) The diagnosis of language disorders in bilingual children: Surface-oriented and pragmatic criteria. *Journal of Speech and Hearing Disorders* 48, November, 385–94.

Jones, K., King, G., Picton, B. and Vasey, C. (1990) The assessment of bilingual pupils: a way forward? *Education Psychology in Practice*, July, 69–74.

Keating, M.C. (1990) Language contact between Portuguese and English. Unpublished M.Phil. Dissertation. New Hall, Cambridge, UK.

Lehiste, I. (1988) *Lectures in Language Contact*. MIT Press.

Linguistic Minorities Project – LMP (1985) In M. Stubbs (ed.) *The Other Languages of England*. Routledge and Kegan Paul.

Mayone Dias, E. (1986) O Portinglês. *Peregrinação – Artes e Letras da Diáspora*

Portuguesa 3 (11) 4–9.

Ormerod. J. (1982) *Sunshine, Moonlight*. Harmondsworth: Picture Puffins, Penguin Books Ltd.

Poplack, S. (1980) Sometimes I'll start a sentence in Spanish y termino en Español: Towards a typology of code-switching. *Linguistics* 1, 581–618.

Santarita P. and Martin-Jones, M. (1991) The Portuguese speech community. In S. Alladina and V. Edwards (eds) *Multilingualism in the British Isles*. Longman Linguistics Library.

Weinreich, U. (1953) *Languages in Contact: Findings and Problems*. Mouton Publishers.

Winer, B.J. (1971) *Statistical Principles in Experimental Design* (2nd edn). New York: McGraw-Hill.

8 A Resource for Assessing the Language Skills of Bilingual Pupils

MIKE HAWORTH AND JOHN JOYCE

'Children's abilities on entry to school were rarely systematically assessed and even in those few schools where assessment was undertaken, often no use was made of this information to plan the future programmes of work'

' . . . no school provided a systematic programme of oracy targeted to the needs of any individual or group.'

OFSTED (1992)

Introduction/Background

The development of the 'bilingual language record', which is described below, emerged from the Section 11 funded project work of two educational psychologists, looking both at assessment issues with individual black – bilingual children, and city-wide achievement monitoring and action planning for these pupils. The main reasons for designing another language record are outlined in the following sections.

(1) Local education authorities are in continuous receipt of requests for assessment of individual pupils, not only where possible special educational needs (SEN) are being queried, but also where schools are asking how to meet the needs of pupils with limited (but unquantified) English. Assessment in both these contexts has frequently been 'light' vis a vis oracy aspects of language (i.e. listening and speaking as opposed to more literacy-based skills). More information on a child's language, coupled with information on the language demands being made of the child, would encourage a 'hypothesis testing approach': querying a range of provision and context as well as within-child

factors as possible explanations for lack of progress. Moreover, following recent changes in U.K. government regulations on the assessment of special educational needs, there is growing interest in 'learning outcomes' and 'Individual Education Plans', and hence an opportunity to be more specific in respect of oracy.

(2) Wider studies of the achievement of groups of pupils have tended, even more than the above individual assessments, to omit attention to oracy skills. There is growing recognition of the poverty and inadequacy of available information on 'achievement', as assessed, for example, solely by a word-reading 'test'. There is a clear need for better data on oracy skills, as a central component of addressing the issue of what constitutes effective provision and monitoring for bilingual pupils. In relation to first language competence in particular this information is usually non-existent.

Consultation with schools on the above areas of assessment and achievement indicated the need for a language record, which was developed in conjunction with a speech therapist colleague. The aim was to develop a tool which 'fitted' the model being presented in school and centre-based professional development sessions on bilingual language development and assessment.

Rationale

In presenting these training sessions, the following were some of the key points as we saw them. (These should not be seen as 'authoritative' or categorical statements, but as representing our understanding of the state of the current debate.)

(1) Increased emphasis is needed on the primacy of oracy, the key area for bilingual pupils, and on the need to address the paucity of information we have on bilingual pupils' L1 and L2 oracy skills.

(2) A central question needs reframing: The challenge of working with bilingual children is less 'How to teach English?' (although an element of this needs to remain) and more 'How can the curriculum be effectively delivered to pupils who don't have English as their first language?' (See for example the work of Skutnabb-Kangas, 1981, and Fitzpatrick, 1993.) This is an important distinction because it throws the achievement spotlight onto curriculum and effectiveness of provision, not onto pupil or pupil background 'problems'. For some schools (and LEAs) this implies an attitude shift, and a removal of planning for bilingual pupils away from SEN departments (and 'supplementary', e.g. Section 11 funded 'support') to mainstream teachers and subject

departments.

(3) Effective curriculum delivery requires an effective match between pupil 'entry skills' and the teaching objectives, including a 'match' of teacher talk to children's language level. The relationship between these two is dynamic not static, and plans need to be flexible rather than tightly broken down to small teaching steps, as was formerly popular, particularly in the SEN field. In order to assess such entry skills, and evaluate subsequent progress, accurate observation and recording is needed.

(4) A focus is needed on both languages (L1 and L2), which should be seen as complementary, mutually additive, rather than L1 interfering with the acquisition of L2. Acquisition of 'native-like competence' in English is a long, not short term objective; and first language has to be seen as much more than a transitional step. The ideal language medium for a particular task is the language the child is most comfortable with, particularly where new learning is occurring.

(5) Assessment and learning activities should be embedded in meaningful contexts, with the experiences of the child employed. It is here that the Cummins model (Cummins, 1984) can be incorporated to good effect. Successful teachers with bilingual children develop practical language activities, whilst maintaining cognitive challenge and high expectations.

One difficulty we have found with using the Cummins framework in practice for assessment and planning, particularly with reference to language development, is obtaining agreement and precision both in relation to the child's current skill level, and the level of difficulty of the curriculum task(s) set. Many school and support staff do not have sufficiently detailed knowledge about the children's language proficiency, and background, nor do they have a tool for analysing the language demands of the work set. Hence the need for a running language 'record' to structure observations and language aspects of topic planning.

Overview of the Record

(1) The language record is a 'context-based' device, focusing on what children are actually doing in the classroom, rather than being an abstract, i.e. non-contextual, 'test' of language functioning removed from the curriculum. It moves away from norm referenced assessment, the disadvantages of which, particularly with bilingual pupils, have been well catalogued elsewhere – for example by Desforges (1982). However, any assessment device needs to be regarded with caution,

and any suggestion that the 'perfect device' has been produced taken none too seriously (see Cline, 1993). No claim of perfection is made with regard to the record described here.

(2) It incorporates both L1 and L2, providing a picture of 'overall language development', not just English as a Second Language in isolation. It has particular relevance for the early years and primary sector, and is relevant for all children, not just children with SEN.

(3) Its aim is to inform the planning of teaching, emphasising oracy aspects of language, particularly language 'use' rather than 'understanding'. (Analysis of both, in two languages, can become very unwieldy.) This is not to diminish the vital importance of effective listening and comprehension. But a working assumption is being made that in most cases use indicates comprehension.

(4) The aim is to sample language, rather than produce an impossibly long checklist, and to adhere to an approximately developmental sequence, including various aspects of language, and yet seeking to maintain relevance for classroom use. Analysis of language use remains time consuming, but the time taken is significantly reduced once staff become familiar with the record.

Description/Format

There are four main components to the record, and accompanying notes.

(1) The **Child Information** section mirrors the stress on the importance of collecting accurate background information recommended by Desforges (1982), Cline & Frederickson (1991) and others. It is not substantially different from other background information proformas, but we are still often surprised that some schools and teachers (and psychologists etc.) do not have information about children that should be fundamental to assessment and programme planning. The question 'What is the child's own experience as a language learner?' is, unfortunately, one which is too often left unanswered.

Examples of and brief rationale for items from this section:

Languages used (make a note of where and with whom used).

Name and age of siblings (included because a child with older siblings already attending school is likely to have had more exposure to English through them than a child without older siblings.)

Are there affective factors which may have affected language development? (e.g. motivation, confidence, attitudes to learning). One example is that more outgoing, extrovert children are likely to en-

engage earlier in social interactions and hence have more opportunity to practice their listening and speaking skills.

(2) The **Functions** section ('uses' of language by the child) was developed as an elaboration of the BOLD oral language inventory (Mattes & Omark, 1984) and Joan Tough's work on children's use of language (Tough, 1976). It is designed to relate directly to children's use of language in the classroom. This section is subdivided as follows:

Language behaviours

'Here and now' language

Describing and clarifying less immediate experiences

Planning actions/ Directing actions

Language of imagination

Abstract use of language/Reasoning

This has proved to be the section of the assessment device that teachers completed most often. Spaces have been left for users to add their own items. Examples of items from this section:

2.5. Maintains concrete topic (early conversational skill).
The child is able to maintain a discussion, in context, over several utterances during interaction with peers.

3.1. Describes events from recent past.
The child is able to give an accurate account of personal recent experiences

5.1. Expresses imagination based on real life.
The child uses language to express imagination which develops from actual events or situations.

(3) The **Structures** section is a simplification of the developmental sequence and structures described by Wells (1985), Crystal (1976), and by Knowles & Masidlover (1982). This the 'easiest' section to map out, and easiest on which to 'score' children. It allows for a 'rough and ready' but speedy comparison to be made between two of the languages a child is learning to use.

Examples of items from this section:

1. One word utterances
   e.g. 'no', 'me', 'drink', 'geroff', 'brmm brmm', 'moo'.

6. Complex sentences, with subordinate clauses
   e.g. 'The boy who hit me ran away'.
   'I'll do it when I've finished dinner'.

(4) For several reasons the **Content** section focuses mainly on verbs. Firstly, the usual list of nouns quickly becomes unwieldy in any inventory. Secondly, most teachers follow the good practice of generating their own lists of nouns for new topics but often overlook consideration of other word classes. Thirdly, we wanted to generate a word list (the verbs) that might be more generally useful and not restricted to particular topics. Verbs, or 'action words', once acquired and used, tend naturally to lead to use of nouns. There is a set of pictures illustrating the verbs on the checklist. There is also a sheet for recording use of 'other speech forms' including adjectives, and prepositions.

Examples of items from this section:

1. Uses 3 or 4 action words, e.g. 'eat', 'drink', 'paint'.

3. Extensive verb vocabulary, including less concrete, more mental activities, e.g. 'imagine', 'understand', 'think'.

5. Use of auxiliary verbs, e.g. 'might', 'must', 'won't'.

(5) The **Language Summary** is an attempt to bring together the various sections of the record and to allow a comparison to be made between language development in two languages. It is a recent revision, and users may prefer to develop their own summary.

Also included in the record are some observation record forms which we hope will encourage users to make some direct observations and to avoid the 'tick box' syndrome which can be encouraged by checklists or recording schedules.

Uses and Applications

In one sense the language record is not solely an assessment device, but aims to help 'shape' curriculum delivery and assessment approaches used with children. That is to say, we hope that in some ways it will inform teachers in the way that they plan curriculum delivery for, and consider the assessment of, children who are learning two (or more) languages. We would expect the language record to be adapted quickly by teachers and others to reflect more precisely their own requirements. We would also be surprised if the whole record was used on every occasion with every child.

There are several different ways of using the record. The two main applications that are envisaged are (i) for school staff as well as 'outside' support staff (e.g. agencies helping with assessment) to focus on the needs of individual pupils, and (ii) as part of a school's internal planning or review of language provision for a class or group of children.

For assessment of an individual pupil

The record may be used to aid identification of an individual pupil's progress, and the planning of teaching. It is important, however, that the items on the record form are not regarded as a 'language curriculum' through which children should be 'forced'. This is contrary to the principles mentioned above.

It can be used to structure observations made in class or in a one-to-one interview with a child, and in this way help in collecting information on the basis of which to test hypotheses about a child's lack of educational progress. (For example, is lack of educational progress due to an overall language difficulty or limited English acquisition?) For more details see the chapter on hypothesis testing by Anna Wright in the UCL training pack (Cline & Frederickson, 1991).

The best person to use the record would be a bilingual teacher. However, it is possible to have two people working together. One method trialled by the authors (neither of whom can speak non-European languages) is to use probes in English first, and then for a bilingual colleague to use L1. Rather than letting a child struggle with English responses, a bilingual person should step in and use the probe in L1 if the child is not responding in L2.

The record can be used flexibly – e.g. filling in as much as possible retrospectively from existing knowledge of the child, then checking out 'gaps'. Both audio recording and transcribing of children's talk can be used, but these are time consuming and transcribing needs a good deal of practice before a degree of proficiency is reached.

Case studies (extracts from fuller assessments)

Ahsan was referred by his school at age 6, with a query as to whether he had special educational needs (SEN) or 'special needs' arising from having English as a second language (or both). With the help of a bilingual worker in the school, a record was made of language used by the child both in group situations in class, and in 1:1 interview (using prepared 'probes' to add to the language observed more naturally in class). Analysis with the record suggested that Ahsan used mainly single words in English, largely restricted to reporting on 'Here and now' events; and many of these words were in imitation rather than spontaneous utterances. In his first language he was stringing together simple sentences, and able to report on less immediate experiences (for example what he had done when he had got up that morning).

In conjunction with observation of other aspects of his functioning in class, and discussion of his strengths with parents (good attention skills, interest in books, established early numeracy skills etc.) the hypothesis was made that 'SEN-type' learning difficulties were much less a factor than lack of experience and use of English. Recommendations included: (a) continued use of first language, particularly for 'new' learning, looking in particular at more extended and connected narratives (e.g. description of story in his own words; and (b) continued modelling in English of simple sentences related to current play, organised in a mixed-language group context. A sample of group language activities, derived from earlier 'workshops' were sent as exemplars.

Ahmed was a later entrant to school, and referred at age 9+, but with a similar query. For Ahmed no access was obtained to a bilingual English/ L1 worker (Arabic) in school. In a meeting with the family, an aunt attended who was fluent in both languages, and so questions were asked to try elicit the relative use of and competence in English and Arabic in different contexts. The picture emerging was that Ahmed uses only English in the school, but both English and Arabic at home. The family view was that competence in English and Arabic was very comparable; and that he was a bright boy whose understanding was better than his use of language.

In classroom observation considerable difficulty was noted in Ahmed's attending to teacher talk in large group situations. (He fiddled, yawned, looked elsewhere, etc.) During a subsequent one hour interview with Ahmed, during which his attention and concentration were very good, English language skills were probed, using the record, along with an audio-recording. 'Here and Now language' was competent but not 'Less Immediate' (past or future) events (including difficulty with verb tense); and his ability to share a book or picture was also limited. Ahmed tended to itemise peripheral aspects of illustrations, rather than sequence the key events. His talk contained some co-ordinated sentences, but there were also disjointed utterances, with parts of speech omitted, and a lot of hesitancy. He spoke quietly but quickly. Recommendations included individual and small group work on 'sharing' texts, emphasising continuity/connected narrative. A suggestion/request has been made to the family that some utterances in Arabic are recorded at home, describing a book and pictures, and sent to us for comparison with English.

For group, class or school use

There are many considerations to take into account when planning at class or group level. (See Figure 8.1 below.)

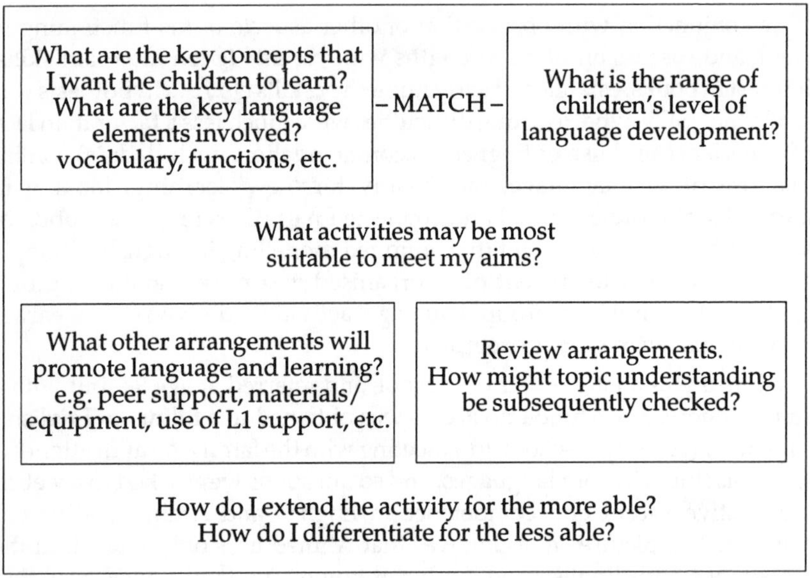

What are the key concepts that I want the children to learn? What are the key language elements involved? vocabulary, functions, etc.

– MATCH –

What is the range of children's level of language development?

What activities may be most suitable to meet my aims?

What other arrangements will promote language and learning? e.g. peer support, materials/ equipment, use of L1 support, etc.

Review arrangements. How might topic understanding be subsequently checked?

How do I extend the activity for the more able? How do I differentiate for the less able?

Figure 8.1

At the early stages of planning, when a new topic is being prepared, the record can be used to match the known 'language levels' of the target group to the linguistic demand of the teacher's curriculum objectives. In class or group planning a fundamental question to ask is, 'Am I expecting work which is beyond the pupils in terms of their level of English language?' Some teachers reported that they have found it easier to use the 'functions' section of the language record rather than the Cummins' framework to try to help answer this question. The value of the Cummins framework for our work on language has been the emphasis on context. However, the record asks specific questions, whereas the Cummins framework is unspecific in terms of content. Teachers can have difficulty placing items on the framework; perhaps in part because the dichotomy between level of cognitive difficulty and context embeddedness is to some extent artificial, especially in relation to listening and speaking skills.

As the items on the functions list appertain to activities in class, programme planning should be easier. Even though the items in the functions section were developed in collaboration with many practising teachers, individual teachers may find that adding to or amending items will make it more useful for them.

The record (or parts of the record) can also be used for monitoring of group progress. It makes more possible a longitudinal study of educational achievement, including oracy as well as literacy, linked with educational outcomes. (Which pupils do best? Can their earlier language achievements be replicated by other pupils?). It could also help with action research within a school. The response of several local schools to a recent achievement survey has been to identify the need for a 'baseline' assessment of pupils' language on entry to nursery and reception classes.

Possible Developments

Adding vocabulary and language functions

The authors' intention is that schools will add their own vocabulary items, and language functions that they think are important but which are not included in the record; then develop and adapt their own language activities, matched to current classroom topics.

Both within a school and across schools a resource bank of activities, ideas and materials for fostering talk is needed, matched closely with National Curriculum Attainment targets. In this respect the 'networking' work of the Collaborative Learning Project (see reference in the bibliography) is to be particularly recommended.

Contributing to school INSET

The record could be used to contribute to school INSET. Its use can encourage staff to be confident in identifying and meeting language needs without reliance on 'outside expertise'. It can help staff appreciate that they do not need 'special' apparatus for language work. The authors have incorporated the record in sessions on bilingualism and language assessment both for colleagues within the special services section of the LEA, and for mainstream school staff, using the UCL training pack (Cline & Frederickson, 1991), and video recordings of children's talk. Particularly fruitful have been workshops run to prompt the writing of practical language activities.

It is here that the Cummins framework is most directly applicable, heightening a focus on oracy, within the context of the current classroom topic. The key is to link the focus on functions with interventions and teaching practice more generally. Practical activities which teaching staff and bilingual assistants have developed through such workshops have included: group design of, and role play with, mannikins (to fit with the action vocabulary for an ongoing class topic on 'My Body'); and manufacture of 'stick puppets' to accompany rewriting of (monocultural) traditional stories (such as Goldilocks) with characters and materials better matching the pupils' backgrounds.

This type of bilingual record cannot 'stand alone'. It is inseparable from a wider positive attitude and policy towards fostering children's language including usage of first language. Otherwise there is a danger that this type of 'assessment' tool will focus too much on the child, drawing attention away from the provision, including the curriculum.

'Probes' for obtaining language samples

For staff less familiar with a child, and with less time in class, it helps to have a set of 'probes' for obtaining language samples, particularly for the 'Functions' section. (This also allows for more consistency between observers). Several probes may be needed for particular items in the record, in case early ones do not work (i.e. 'failure' on an item may be because the probe doesn't work, rather than because the child lacks language proficiency). The authors have begun to collate some probes. These are at an early stage of trialling; and many users will be able to develop their own in addition.

The full record, and accompanying handbook, is available from the authors at Leeds Special Services, The Blenheim Centre, Crowther Place, Leeds LS6 2ST. It is intended as part of an ongoing debate on assessment and provision for bilingual pupils. It will certainly need modification after further use. (Constructive feedback would be welcomed). But even as it stands it has been found to be helpful for both individual child and wider 'systems' work.

Appendix: The Bilingual Language Assessment Record

THE BILINGUAL LANGUAGE

ASSESSMENT RECORD

INTRODUCTION

The bilingual language assessment record is an attempt to structure some of our observations and thoughts on children's language development. It is not intended to be a perfect measure of a child's language development, but a device to shape the process of gathering information to help, for example, to inform decisions about language support for a particular child. It is envisaged that later versions will include suggestions to help foster language development.

The record provides a structure for school and nursery staffs' observation and recording of young, or older recent entrant bilingual children's language development in English and their first language. It focuses on oracy, listening and speaking, not literacy aspects of language. It uses a very broad breakdown of language into function, structure, and vocabulary.

RATIONALE FOR THIS BILINGUAL ASSESSMENT RECORD

The record aims to address the current paucity of information on bilingual children's language development, as individuals and as groups, and to serve as a tool for those committed to promoting these children's language development, as one key aspect of enhancing their subsequent educational achievement.

The record aims to put the focus back onto oracy, in a context of massive educational change where some of this focus may have been lost or swamped. It begins from the premise that bilingual children have particular needs in an educational setting which is predominantly monolingual. Perhaps a more accurate way of stating this is that the staff, the curriculum providers, have particular challenges to face. The children need to have full access to the broad curriculum, whilst also acquiring English as a second language. These English language needs are not to be confused with special educational needs. On the contrary children who are learning more than one language should be seen as an asset, having special skills as bilinguals.

It is based on the premise that L1 and L2 are interdependent. They have an additive not an 'interference' effect on each other, such that children whose first language is promoted, rather than merely being assisted to acquire English, will be more competent users of English.

It provides a basis for a 'value-added' assessment of individuals' and groups' progress, enabling progress to be monitored longitudinally and measured - e.g. at the end of Key Stage 1 against 'entry' skills.

1

The intention of focusing on particular language details is not to over-emphasise subsequent 'teaching' of those 'bits' of language that are missing, as some sort of isolated language activity. Language is best learnt as part of meaningful and interesting activities and interactions with others, rather than by rote learning or 'drill'.

DESCRIPTION

Language constitutes a highly complex range of inter-related skills. At some (inevitable) risk of oversimplification, the record breaks down language functioning into 3 main aspects:

I   THE USES MADE OF LANGUAGE (FUNCTIONS)
How and for what purposes does the child use talk (a.in L1; b. in English)? For example, does the child ask questions, or give a running commentary on her own actions. Is she stuck in the present or can she talk about past and future or imaginary events?

II THE LANGUAGE STRUCTURES USED
Does the child speak mainly in single words, (a. in L1; b. in English) or are simple, even complex sentences being used?

III THE VOCABULARY CONTENT
How extensive is the child's vocabulary (in L1; in English)?
To make this section more manageable, and to reflect the importance of these words, a decision was made to prioritise verbs here - rather than list lots of object names or labels.

Each of these areas is set out in a (roughly) developmental format, with skills normally acquired earlier appearing first. There is not however any sequence implied from one area to the next (although some of the language behaviours in I will occur first before any structures and vocabulary).

USING THE RECORD

i) Which children?
The record is not intended for use with all children, nor with all bilingual children (although more information on all children's language development is needed). It is better suited for use with a sample of children (eg those bilingual children on whom a language support worker has been asked to focus). On the other hand it is not seen as restricted to 'bilingual' in the narrow sense of, for example, Punjabi-English speaking children. The language needs of children from an African-Caribbean background, or a monolingual 'white UK' background could also be addressed through the record, where it is possible to 'focus' on a few children.

It may be that the sample of children for whom you wish to use the record is pre-selected anyway (eg where bilingual children are in a small minority in the school, or where a decision has already been made as to which children to focus on, following discussion between staff).

If however the initial task is to reduce the sample size/ identify a target group for a more intensive language focus, then the following initial steps may be found helpful:

1. Collect samples of a child's utterances in L1 and L2 - sampling several different learning and social contexts.
   - See attached 'Language Record' sheet.

2. Compare the results with samples obtained from same-age bilingual peers. Analysis at this screening level cannot be detailed; note however whether the child is predominantly using single words, or more complex utterances; and whether the child is mainly reporting on (possibly simply 'labelling') 'here and now' events/ objects, or using language more adventurously, for example, to direct others, describe more remote events or express imagination.

In making comparisons however note the following:
   - The number of terms the child has had in school and nursery, compared with peers.
   - Whether or not there are siblings at home (especially older siblings who have use of English)
   - Any known 'emotional'/ personality and background factors (eg. family stresses) which may result in the child being more reticent, without necessarily reflecting less competent language proficiency.

3. Retain the (dated) language samples on all the children as a basis for reviewing progress at future dates. (Recordings/ transcription of samples of child utterances -eg using a tape recorder - are invaluable as a baseline against which to measure subsequent progress, even without any detailed 'analysis' of content.)
Identify those children for whom a more detailed assessment of language using the fuller record would be particularly helpful.

4. Consider, in light of the initial language sample, whether you wish to focus within the record on one particular area as a priority or starting point. (If the child has an extensive vocabulary you may wish to omit the vocabulary area altogether, or use your own 'key words' relating to current classroom topics).

ii) When to use?
   The record is particularly designed to act as a longitudinal record of language progression, not a one-off assessment. Once familiarity with the record is acquired it is not expected that school staff would spend an hour or more observing and filling it in on a child. It is particularly suitable for beginning with younger children (Nursery/reception) and maintaining up into Key Stage 2 (and beyond if a child is having particular difficulties in English or L1).

However if begun soon after 'entry' of the child into an educational setting, it should be recognised that a settling in phase, even extended 'silent phase' can be expected for many bilingual children entering a predominantly monolingual school.

ADMINISTRATION

The record works best when it is used by adults who are familiar with the child, for example a teacher or language co-ordinator working in close co-operation with bilingual support staff. (Note that it should not be assumed that a bilingual staff are 'experts' in bilingual language assessment, any more than white monolingual staff would be seen as experts in assessment of a child's English language).

COLLECTING BACKGROUND INFORMATION

Attention should be given to collection of good background information on the child, with parents as one of the most important sources. This information should cover not only what languages the child uses in what settings, but also what siblings there are and what their use of English is like.

It should be recognised and recorded that for many children 'bi'-lingual is an underestimate of the number of languages the child is exposed to and using. (For example a child in addition to Punjabi and English may be learning the Koran in Arabic and attending literacy schooling in Urdu.)

Observations are best recorded while a child is relaxed and at ease. Wherever possible it is hoped that the language items included in the record can be assessed through observing 'natural' language occurring, rather than through artificial 'testing'(although some of the vocabulary items in particular may be more rapidly checked via a battery of prepared pictures or objects).

Experienced teachers and other staff will know in what situations language most readily 'flows' from particular children. For newer staff it may be worth spelling out what some of these good language settings and activities are; what are some of the best stimuli and how to elicit language in an 'open-ended' way, following the child's lead and not using a set of 'closed' questions. Children should be observed in several different contexts (see the useful grid in the Primary Language Record), and by several different staff as well as parents, so that a range of observations is gathered.

RECORDING

Most of the recording on the forms is straight forward. The easiest way of using the records is to write down examples of the language the child is using in the appropriate box. For example, if the child has said 'I got a big ball' this should be noted on the 'Structures' form in the row headed 'simple sentences' under L2.

The exceptions to this are the 'verbs' section where it is suggested that you enter the date against verbs that you have heard the child use, and the 'functions' section which has a simple scoring system. As with any such scoring system it is difficult to be accurate and individual teachers or school staffs will establish their own meaning for these scores or develop their own scoring system. As the record is meant to be a longitudinal one it is important that items recorded are dated or coded, perhaps by colour.

It should also be noted that the structure of the record is 'led' by the English language and there will be times when utterances produced in a child's first language do not fit easily into this structure.

ACKNOWLEDGEMENTS

The authors are indebted to Dr J. Reynolds, Speech Therapy Services manager, for his invaluable help in designing the record; also to Leeds' teachers and bilingual workers for their feedback on early versions.

Child information which has assessment implications

Child's name:

Date of Birth: Child's class:

Languages used (make a note of where and with whom used)

Previous education (including schooling outside UK, and nursery, with dates)

Has the child had extra help/support with English? (note details)

Has the child had any breaks in their education (e.g. extended trips abroad)?

Name and age of siblings

Are there any affective factors which may have affected language development? (eg. motivation, confidence, attitudes to learning)

What is the family's view of the child's development ?

Have there been any health/medical factors affecting development?

Is the child attending supplementary/religious schools? What progress is being made there?

Are there any factors in the school environment which support or hinder the child's language learning?

LANGUAGE FUNCTION INVENTORY

Name   Date

Indicate in the appropriate column and row the child's level of competence for each item by entering 1 (=emerging) 2 (=developing competence) 3 (=competence). If there is no evidence of the child having achieved an item leave it blank. Enter the child's first (L1) and second (L2) language above the columns.

	L1	L2
1. Language Behaviours		
1. Maintains eye contact. *The child will look at and maintain eye contact for at least 5 seconds with another person.*		
2. Attends to speaker. *The child looks at the speaker when spoken to and maintains eye contact whilst being spoken to.*		
3. Gains listeners attention. *The child is able to gain attention by verbal or non-verbal means.*		
4. Is able to take turns. *The child is able to act/ speak and wait whilst others act/speak.*		
5. Follows directions. *The child follows simple directions in the classroom.*		
6. Initiates interactions. *The child initiates conversations with classmates.*		
Space for user to add own items		
2. 'Here and now' language		
1. Uses gestures (e.g. pointing) to express basic needs. *This may include leading by the hand, tugging, waving, etc..*		
2. Expresses basic needs (e.g. "I want", "give me"). *The child can inform others of personal needs.*		
3. Asks for help in the classroom. *The child is able to ask for help with classwork.*		

	L1	L2
4. Uses play talk. *This may begin with a simple brmm brmm, woof woof etc. and progress to play the role of the shopkeeper or customer in the class shop.*		
5. Maintains concrete topic (early conversational skill). *The child is able to maintain a discussion, in context, over several utterances during interactions with peers.*		
6. Suggests what to do next in a practical activity.		
7. Gives running commentary on own actions. *This may not necessarily be to an audience, it may be the child talking to her/himself.*		
8. Asks for and gives information on immediate environment e.g. 'what's this', 'who's that'.		
3. Describing and clarifying less immediate experiences		
1. Describes events from recent past. *The child is able to give an accurate account of recent personal experiences.*		
2. Describes events with a simple sequence. *The child describes a sequence of events (with 2 or 3 parts to the sequence) in the order in which they occurred.*		
3. Answers less concrete questions (e.g. when, how, why).		
4. Asks 'when', 'how', 'why' questions.		
5. Describes simple future events (e.g. I'm going to...). *The child is able to relate simple intentions or predictions e.g. "it's going to rain".*		

	L1	L2
6. Listens to and discusses new topic. *The child should be able to manage this for a* *sustained period.*		
4. Planning actions/directing actions		
1. Follows a sequence of instructions. *The child can follow accurately a sequence of 2* *or 3 consecutive instructions.*		
2. Describes solutions. *The child can describe solutions for simple* *problems.*		
3. Describes plans. *The child describes plans for a future event or* *activity.*		
4. Describes a sequence. *The child describes a sequence of events (with 3* *or more parts to the sequence) in the order in* *which they occurred.*		
5. Directs other people. *The child uses language to direct others' actions* *e.g. gives instructions.*		
5. Language of imagination		
1. Expresses imagination based on real life. *The child uses language to express imagination* *which develops from actual events or situations.*		
2. Expresses imagination based on fantasy. *The child is able to express imaginative ideas* *with very little contextual support.*		
3. Develops a story. *The child is able to use language to build upon a* *story that they have heard/read.*		

	L1	L2
4. Listens to stories/poems and talks about them. *E.g. the child talks about the characters in a story or what they liked/disliked about it.*		
6. Abstract use of language/Reasoning		
1. Supports viewpoints. *The child expresses personal opinions and is able to supply arguments to support those opinions.*		
2. Justifies own behaviour. *The child is able to supply an argument to support their actions e.g. give an excuse.*		
3. Uses language for prediction. *The child is able to give an explanation for a predicted event e.g. say why something is likely to happen.*		
4. Articulates feelings. *The child uses language to express emotions such as anger, fear, or joy.*		
5. Asks more probing/hypothetical questions. *E.g. asks 'what if...' or 'how about...' questions.*		

SENTENCES AND GRAMMATICAL STRUCTURES

Indicate in the appropriate box the child's level of competence for each item and each language by entering 1 (= emerging) 2 (= developing competence) 3 (= competence). Consider the child's use of and understanding of language. Make a note of any observations you make in the corresponding box on the opposite page.

	L1	L2
1. One word utterances e.g. 'no' 'me' 'drink' 'dog' 'geroff' 'brmm brmm' 'moo'		
2. Putting two words together not just stereo-typed utterances such as 'all-gone', 'bye-bye' which are in most respects one word utterances. Examples can be intended as a statement or a question (for example, 'daddy gone' - 'daddy gone?'). e.g. 'eat bun' 'me bath' 'mummy sock' 'spoon floor' 'hit teddy'		
3. Use of 'phrase' (at least two words) Noun or verb modified by another word. e.g. 'big ball' 'don't like' 'pick up' 'my new car' 'going to fall' 'under bed'.		
4. Simple sentence Longer, 5 or 6 word, utterances, complete with subject and verb as appropriate. Fewer telegraphic deletions e.g. 'me go (to) shop'. Can include questions, who, why when etc.. e.g. 'I got a big ball' 'Where's my mummy's car?' 'That big boy fell down at school'		
5. Coordinated Sentences Narrative with sentences joined together with 'but / or / and / then' etc.. Examples would not include pairs of words joined together e.g. 'Janet and John', 'fish and chips' e.g. 'I went home and I had a drink and I played trains.' 'He got up then he went downstairs then he had breakfast'. 'I looked in the garden but I couldn't find it'. 'We might watch T.V. or we might play shops'.		
6. Complex sentences With subordinate clauses. e.g.'The boy who hit me ran away'. 'I'll do it when I've finished dinner'. 'If he comes I'll tell him what happened'. 'I like chocolate because it gives me energy'.		

Sentence and grammatical structures
(notes and observations)

1. One word utterances

2. Putting two words together

3. Use of 'phrase'

4. Simple sentences

5. Coordinated sentences

6. Complex sentences

LANGUAGE CONTENT / VOCABULARY

The focus in this section is on verbs. The assumption is that if these are occurring, object words will also be in use. Record actual words used rather than 'scoring' as in earlier sections.

L1	L2
1. Uses 3 or 4 action words e.g. 'eat' 'drink' 'sit' 'paint'.	
2. Wider range of 15 - 20 verbs (See list overleaf).	
3. Extensive verb vocabulary, including less concrete, more mental activities e.g. 'imagine' 'understand' 'think'.	
4. Use of phrasal verbs e.g. 'fall down' 'get up' 'turn over' 'put away'.	
5. Use of auxiliary verbs e.g. 'might' 'must' 'won't'.	
6. Use of past and future tense forms.	

VOCABULARY - VERBS

Early verbs

can	have (has, had)	sit
come	is (was)	stop
drink	like	want
eat	look	
get (got)	put	
give	run	
go (gone, going)	see	

Wider range of verbs

blow	hold	stick
break	imagine	swim
brush	jump	take
bring	kick	taste
build	laugh	think
buy	lie (down)	throw
clap	listen	touch
climb	love	turn
colour	make	understand
cook	open	walk
crawl	paint	wash
cry	play	watch
cut	point	write
dance	pour	
dig	pretend	
drive	pull	
drop	push	
dry	read	
fall (down)	ride	
feel	roll	
find	show	
fold	sing	
hear	sleep	
hit	speak	

USE OF OTHER SPEECH FORMS

Note down examples of the child's language in the appropriate boxes below

L1	L2
1.Use of simple adjectives (size, colour, shape etc.)	
2.Use of simple prepositions (in, on, under, etc.)	
3.Use of pronouns (me, it, her, etc.)	
4. Use of adverbs (slowly, quickly, quietly, etc.)	

● Haworth Joyce Leeds City Council 1994

17

LANGUAGE RECORD SHEET

Context / Activity	Language
In this column make a note of the activity the child is engaged in, the setting, which other people are present and what language the child is responding to. Attempt to make a note of what you consider to be important elements of the child's environment when the language sample is being taken.	In this column attempt to make a record of what the child is saying. Make sure it is clear which language the child is using.

LANGUAGE SUMMARY

This summary sheet may be used in a number of different ways to compare children's L1 and L2 development e.g. dates, ticks, colour coded .....

Language functions	L1	L2	Language structures	L1	L2	Content (verbs)	L1	L2
1.Language behaviours			1.One word utterances			1.Uses 3 or 4 action e.g.'eat 'drink' 'sit' 'paint'		
2.'Here and now' language			2.Putting two words together			2.Wider range of 15-20 verbs		
3.Describing and clarifying less immediate experiences			3.Use of 'phrase'			3.Extensive verb vocabulary		
4.Planning actions/ directing actions			4.Simple sentences			4.Use of phrasal verbs		
5.Language of imagination			5.Coordinated sentences			5.Use of auxiliary verbs		
6.Abstract use of language/reasoning			6.Complex sentences			6.Use of past and future tense forms		

● Haworth Joyce Leeds City Council 1994   19

References

Cline, T. (1993) Educational assessment of bilingual pupils: Getting the context right. *Educational and Child Psychology* 10 (4), 59–68.

Cline, T. and Frederickson, N. (1991) *Bilingual Pupils and the National Curriculum: Overcoming Difficulties in Teaching and Learning.* London: University College.

Collaborative Learning Project. Stuart Scott, Project Director, 17 Barford Street, London Nl OQB.

Crystal, D., Fletcher, P. and Garman, M. (1976) *The Grammatical Analysis of Language Disability: A Procedure for Assessment and Remediation.* London: Edward Arnold.

Cummins, J. (1984) *Bilingualism and Special Education: Issues in Assessment and Pedagogy.* Clevedon: Multilingual Matters.

Desforges, M. (1982) Assessment of bi-cultural, bi-lingual children. *Association of Educational Psychologists Journal* 5, (10), 7–12.

Fitzpatrick, B. (1993) *The Linguistic Background to ESL.* Paper given at Bradford Conference on ESL.

Knowles, W. and Masidlover, M. (1982) *The Derbyshire Language Scheme.* Derbyshire County Council.

Mattes, L.J. and Omark, D.R. (1984) Bilingual oral language inventory. In *Speech and Language Assessment for the Bilingual Handicapped.* San Diego, CA: College Hill Press.

OFSTED. (1992) *Access and Achievement in Urban Education.* London: HMSO.

Skutnabb-Kangas, T. (1981) *Bilingualism or Not: The Education of Minorities.* Clevedon: Multilingual Matters.

Tough, J. (1976) *Listening to Children Talking.* Schools Council Publications. London: Ward Lock Educational.

Wells, C.G. (1985) *Language Development in the Pre-School Years.* Cambridge: Cambridge University Press.

Glossary

Phrases Associated with the National Curriculum in the U.K.

1993 Education Act

A law passed by the U.K. Parliament which introduced radical reforms to the education system in England and Wales, including new arrangements for overseeing the National Curriculum.

Attainment Target

Attainment Targets provide objectives for what is to be learned in each school subject by the end of each stage of schooling. Attainment targets in each subject are abbreviated, according to number, as AT1, AT2, etc.

Dearing Proposals

The form of National Curriculum and assessment arrangements introduced in 1988 proved very onerous for schools. The Government commissioned Sir Ron Dearing to review the system. His report was published in 1993 and is largely being implemented.

National Curriculum

The United Kingdom has a subject-based National Curriculum. There are three core subjects (English, mathematics and science) and seven other foundation subjects (art, geography, history, music, physical education, technology, and a modern foreign language).

Programme of Study

A Programme of Study (POS) specifies essential teaching within a subject area. POSs have been defined as the matters, skills and processes which must be taught so that pupils meet the objectives set out in the attainment targets.

Statement of Attainment

The Attainment Targets are fairly broad. The Statements of Attainment represent more precise objectives which relate to one of ten levels of attainment that span the whole age range of compulsory schooling.

146

Phrases Associated with the Organisation of Schooling in the U.K.

HMI

Her Majesty's Inspectorate – a body of inspectors of schools that is intended to be independent of both central and local government.

Key Stages

The four phases of compulsory schooling in a child's life:

Key Stage 1	5–7 years	(KS1)
Key Stage 2	8–11 years	(KS2)
Key Stage 3	12–14 years	(KS3)
Key Stage 4	15–16 years	(KS4)

Local Education Authority

The committee of locally elected councillors which is responsible for the organisation and delivery of state-funded education in an area.

Nursery Class/School

Provision for early years education – 2–5 years.

OFSTED

Office of Standards in Education. A recently created body of school inspectors – inheritor of the mantle of HMI.

Primary School

School for children aged 5–11 years, which may also include nursery age children.

SCAA

School Curriculum and Assessment Authority. The national body responsible for advising the government on the National Curriculum and on assessment and examinations.

Secondary School

School for children aged 11–18.

Section 11

A special government fund that was originally set up to support services in areas with a high level of immigration from the British Commonwealth. In this book the term Section 11 has generally been used to refer to teaching provision funded in this way, mainly for teaching English to children whose families do not speak English at home.